The Republic of Letters

Librarian of Congress Daniel J. Boorstin on

Books, Reading, and Libraries

1975–1987

Edited by
JOHN Y. COLE
Director, The Center for the Book

Library of Congress

Washington

1989

Supported in part by the Verner W. Clapp Publications Fund

Library of Congress Cataloging-in-Publication Data

Boorstin, Daniel J. (Daniel Joseph), 1914–
    The republic of letters.

    1. Books and reading.   2. Libraries.   I. Cole,
John Young, 1940–   . II. Title.
Z1003.B735 1988   028′.9   88-600451
ISBN 0-8444-0629-5

∞ The paper used in this publication meets the requirements for
permanence established by the American National Standard for
Information Sciences "Permanence of Paper for Printed Library
Materials" (ANSI Z39.48-1984).

Contents

Contents

Introduction

For twelve years, from 1975 to 1987, Daniel J. Boorstin, a writer and a historian, served as Librarian of Congress. One of his principal goals, he explained in an early interview, was to bring "the perspective of a historian" to the job and to the Library itself.

In this self-appointed task Librarian Boorstin succeeded admirably, never failing to add fresh dimensions or broader perspectives to the customary duties of the Librarian of Congress. Of more immediate significance was the unprecedented way that Daniel Boorstin increased the Library's public visibility. When, in late 1986, he announced that he was going to step down as Librarian, a *New York Times* reporter called the post of Librarian of Congress "perhaps the leading intellectual public position in the nation." It was Boorstin's insistence on a vigorous public role for the Library, which he saw as "an open national library taking all knowledge for its province and a whole nation for its audience" that made such a claim possible. To Daniel Boorstin, the Library of Congress was "the world's greatest Multi-Media Encyclopedia" and simultaneously "a symbol and an instrument of a free people."

I was fortunate to be able to work closely with Daniel Boorstin in developing one of his favorite projects, the Center for the Book. Two Boorstin traits are foremost in my memory. The first is his driving curiosity, a search for answers but especially for discovering how things are interrelated. The second is his fascination with language and his high regard for the precise meaning of words. His unquenchable curiosity and respect for words—which help explain his love of reference books!—are evident throughout this selection of writings about books, reading, and libraries. Most of these pieces are examples of yet another Boorstin characteristic: his irrepressible desire to share what he has learned.

Because, as he said, "it awakened in me what the writing of history could be," Edward Gibbon's *The Decline and Fall of the Roman Empire* is one of Daniel Boorstin's favorite books. Like Gibbon, he practices history as a literary art and, he insists, as an amateur. The amateur spirit, Boorstin maintains, is the noblest ideal and one which has special pertinence to the Library of Congress: "I like to think of this as an exploring institution, where each person can go on his own expedition whenever and wherever hopes and curiosity lead."

This volume focuses on one of Daniel Boorstin's passions: the book and its fundamental importance in our lives. Here he vividly and clearly makes a historian's connections among books, libraries, and the wider universe in which we all live, and his insights illuminate our traditional perceptions about the world of books. Many themes from other Boorstin writings are evident, including his love of facts and "the cosmic significance of trivia," his distrust of professionals and bureaucrats, and his belief in the complementarity of technologies, here most often expressed in terms of the Displacive Fallacy. In extolling the book, often with help from a lively anecdote, Librarian of Congress Boorstin is consistent, persistent, optimistic, and, invariably, eloquent.

JOHN Y. COLE
Director
Center for the Book

A Wellspring of Freedom

Remarks of Daniel J. Boorstin at his induction as Librarian of Congress, November 12, 1975

On June 20, 1975, President Gerald R. Ford nominated Daniel J. Boorstin, then senior historian at the Smithsonian Institution, to be Librarian of Congress. Boorstin was confirmed by the Senate on September 26 and took the oath of office as the twelfth Librarian of Congress on November 12, 1975, in a ceremony in the Library's Great Hall. The event took on unusual significance through the presence of not only congressional leaders but also the President and Vice President of the United States, three members of the President's cabinet, and two former Librarians of Congress. The chairman of the Joint Congressional Committee on the Library, Lucien N. Nedzi of Michigan, praised the Library as "a national library that serves all the people of the United States," and so did President Ford.

This remarkable gathering reflected Daniel Boorstin's belief in the symbolic importance of occasion. The ceremony also marked the beginning of a new era of intensive involvement of the Library of Congress in the public life of the nation. Boorstin's remarks, in which he introduced several themes that would characterize his administration, were delivered amid the partitioned clutter of an overcrowded Great Hall. The promise of the forthcoming expansion into the new Madison Building, however, and the presence of so many prominent friends of the Library of Congress made this historic event a hopeful and optimistic inaugural for the Boorstin years.

$\mathcal{M}$R. PRESIDENT, I would like to thank you for having nominated me for this high position and also to thank you for honoring the Library and for symbolizing its national signif-

icance by your presence here today. This is, I believe, the first
time that a President has so personally and so dramatically
expressed his support for all of us who work here.

Mr. Vice President, Mr. Speaker, presiding officers of the
two Houses, you honor the Library by recognizing today the
role of Congress's library in the work of our Republic.

I would like also to thank the Senate for their vote of
confirmation. To the Joint Committee, which is represented
here by Congressman Nedzi, Chairman, and to the Congress
I pledge my unstinting energies.

A happy providence of history has made the Library of
Congress our nation's library. Our first duty is to serve our
country's Senators and Representatives. But this Library is a
place of congress in other senses too. Here gather the thoughts
and words of earlier Americans, and of spokesmen for all
mankind. Here we gather the present to help the future meet
in congress with the past.

Until recently, libraries—and this Library too—have been
monuments almost exclusively to the Word. As monuments
to the immortal written or printed word, our libraries are
"the tombs of such as cannot die."

Within the last century, however, and especially within the
last few decades, this Library has come to bear vivid witness,
in quite new ways, to the power of the Machine. Most
important, of course, have been the new techniques of
photography and of sound recording, which have provided us
here a new national treasure of images and of sound.

While these and other new resources have been proliferating,
the output of printing presses has been multiplying. The items
which our Library receives in a single *day* are more than five
times the whole number of volumes purchased from Thomas
Jefferson in 1815.

Now, by a lucky coincidence, the electronic computer makes
it possible for us to keep track of our gargantuan collections.
Dr. Mumford, my distinguished predecessor who honors us
by his presence here today, ushered our great Library into the
age of automation, and so has helped save us from being

buried under our own treasures. With this computer technology our Congressional Research Service answers some fifteen hundred queries from Members of Congress each day.

Despite all these efforts, we still face the problem of quantity. Here, again, we meet in unfamiliar form the familiar Parking Problem and the Traffic Jam. Our multiplying vehicles of art and thought create Traffic Jams of the Mind.

I pledge my efforts as Librarian to enlist the whole staff of our Library, which is represented here today, in facing this problem, to use all known techniques and to seek new techniques, to keep the traffic of knowledge and of ideas moving freely and swiftly.

But we must not allow ourselves to forget the reasons for all this movement. We must preserve opportunities for the Exploring Spirit. We must keep open those avenues for bold scholarship and adventuring thought which mankind has made and preserved in books. The computer can help us find what we know is there. But the Book remains our symbol and our resource for the unimagined question and the unwelcome answer.

I pledge myself to try to meet this challenge, to try to keep alive and flourishing the tradition of the Book.

In this great Library there are other, everyday challenges, to which I also pledge my efforts. To serve the Congress and the nation we must keep this Library strong, well nourished, and decently housed. If any of our staff must work in ill-ventilated attics or crowded between improvised partitions, their work suffers, along with their self-respect and their respect for this great institution. If we must pile our precious books on the floor, we are failing all those who have preserved them for us. If the beauty of this magnificent building, this temple of knowledge, is defaced, we are all diminished.

This grand building, the neighboring annex, and the Madison Building into which we will be moving soon, all bear witness to the Congress's enlightened and generous understanding of our mission.

To keep this Library strong, the whole American community

of libraries and of learning must be strong. To keep other libraries strong this Library must be strong. And I am happy to see here representatives of the library community in strength. We must rally enlightened citizens everywhere to save and improve our libraries.

In this Library of Congress, every task is important. We fulfill our mission only if our house is kept neat and orderly, if our treasures are well guarded, if our resources are promptly found and cheerfully delivered. We all share the greatness of this capitol of libraries.

I pledge myself to see that our Library remains what Ira Gershwin was moved to call it on a recent visit here—"a shining star and inspiration, worthy of a mighty nation!" Today, when freedom is retreating in other parts, the whole world needs this Library of Congress for a Wellspring of Freedom. With the encouragement of our President, so personally expressed here today, with the continuing support of the Congress whom we primarily serve, with the cooperation of the nation's and the world's libraries, with the imaginative energies of our scholars, writers, composers, artists, and poets, and above all with the devotion and enthusiasm of our 4,600 fellow workers, we will keep this wellspring flowing.

The Tradition of Change

Statement to the Librarian's Task Force on Goals, Organization, and Planning, January 16, 1976

In his confirmation hearings before the U.S. Senate, Boorstin assured Senator Claiborne Pell that he would appoint a task force to review the Library and its activities and make recommendations for needed changes. He presented his Task Force on Goals, Organization, and Planning with a carefully worded charge, broad in scope and ambition yet precise in its details and deadlines, on January 16, 1976, two months after he had taken the oath of office.

$\mathcal{M}$Y FIRST DUTY as twelfth Librarian of Congress is to review the present state of the Library.

(I) *Why we need a review*

A third of a century has passed since the Library last undertook a full-scale, comprehensive review. These decades have been full of momentous change. The activity of government and the reach of legislation have extended beyond precedent. Our nation has suffered the pangs of adjustment after a World War and has been involved in two other wars. In vast territories of the world the free flow of information is obstructed.

We have lived through a technological revolution more intimate and more pervasive than any before. The airplane has displaced the railroad and the steamship for transcontinental and transoceanic travel. Photography, motion pictures, and sound reproduction have been newly elaborated. Television has entered our living rooms and incited new uses for the radio, newspapers, and magazines. Novel forms of book production and reproduction—microform, xerography, and near-print—have multiplied. The disintegration of paper, once only a threat, has become an immediate menace. The computer has suddenly revealed a whole new science and technology for storing and retrieving information. The pace of scientific progress and of accumulating knowledge has quickened. Space exploration has given a new perspective to our maps and to our ways of seeing our nation's place on our planet.

No part of the Library of Congress has been untouched by these transformations. Today hundreds of our staff are engaged in activities never imagined a half-century ago. The traditional activities of our Library—acquisitions, cataloging, helping the nation's libraries, and communicating information to the Congress—have also been reshaped.

At the same time, the size of our Library has multiplied. When Librarian Archibald MacLeish initiated the last full-scale review thirty-five years ago, the Library had a book collection of some 6 million volumes, an annual budget of about $4 million, and a staff of 1,100. Today our book collection has at least trebled and we have added whole new types of materials. Our annual budget is $166 million and our staff numbers 4,600.

During these decades the Library of Congress has been given a vast range of new statutory responsibilities. Our direct services to the Congress—the primary duties of our Library —have been enlarged, made more subtle and more complex by the Legislative Reorganization Act of 1946 and by the Act of 1970 which reshaped the Legislative Reference Service into the present Congressional Research Service. Our legal mandate to serve the blind and physically handicapped has been widened. Our obligations under the copyright law (now and in prospect) are enormously enlarged. Our congressionally authorized assistance to the nation's libraries and to the world of scholarship and of science has been extended, increased, and modernized. Meanwhile, funds provided by generous citizens for the Library of Congress Trust Fund have offered new opportunities to serve literature, music, and the graphic arts.

Plainly the time has come for a review. The arrival of a new Librarian and the near completion of the Madison Building make such a study especially appropriate now.

(II) *The nature and scope of the review*

Therefore I am now commencing a major review of the Library's goals, organization, and planning. This will require close consultation with the Congress, will draw on the suggestions of our staff, and will reach outside for the constructive criticism and imaginative suggestions of all our constituencies. After full study and careful reflection, our conclusions will, I hope, produce a more effective and efficient Library of Congress, better adapted to the needs of the Congress and the nation as we enter our third century. Meanwhile, however, I will not await the completion of the study for urgently needed changes and obviously overdue innovations.

The review will be wide-ranging, free, and imaginative. It will start from our primary duty to serve the Congress. It will take account of those changes in technology, in the nation and in the world, which affect our usefulness to the Congress and our effectiveness as a national library.

To accomplish our purpose we must increase the sense of our staff's participation in the greatness of our Library. We must improve the working environment in order to make service in the Library a more enriching experience. We must do all in our power to ensure that a career in the Library of Congress will be not merely a career of service, but also a career of self-fulfillment.

It is also urgent that we keep in close touch with our constituencies. The Congress first of all. But our other constituencies as well. The review will open new channels of communication between our Library and all our constituencies and help us keep these channels open and free-flowing.

Among the questions which I suggest are the following:

(1) How well are we serving Congress? How can we better serve the Congress?

(2) How well are we serving other government agencies? How should we be serving them?

(3) How well are we serving the nation's libraries? How (within our legal mandate) can we better serve the nation's public libraries, special libraries, research libraries, and other educational institutions?

(4) Are our collections as widely and as fully used as they ought to be, by scholars, scientists, historians, lawyers, social scientists, poets, composers, performers, and members of the business community? How can improved administration, the addition of private and foundation resources, and more widely diffused information about our resources increase our usefulness to creative persons? How can we more effectively encourage research and creativity in the interest of the Congress and the nation?

(5) How have new technological resources increased our opportunities for service to traditional constituencies and opened avenues of service to new constituencies? What can we do that we are not now doing to serve the blind and physically handicapped, to improve the nation's capacity to read and to help instill the habit of reading? How can we better serve the media?

(6) How has new technology shaped our opportunities and our duty to preserve a full record of American civilization in our time?

(7) As the quantity of informational and cultural materials increases, what can we do that we are not now doing to keep the citizen from being overwhelmed by quantity, and to guide the reader and the viewer through the thickening wilderness of printed and graphic matter?

(8) In a period of change in technology and in the legal protection of authors and artists, what can the Library of

Congress and its Copyright Office do "to promote the progress of science and the useful arts?"

(9) In the midst of rapidly changing technology, what can the Library do to preserve and enrich the tradition of the Book?

(10) In a world where many governments censor and restrict publication and inhibit free expression, are we doing everything necessary and appropriate to keep knowledge and information freely flowing into our Library from everywhere? Are we doing well all that we can to provide the Congress and the nation with a fully stocked free marketplace of the nation's and the world's knowledge and ideas? What can we do to make our collections more speedily available?

These are only a few of the questions which we should consider in our review.

(III) *How we shall proceed*

To advise me in my review of the Library, on January 16, I appointed a staff Task Force on Goals, Organization, and Planning. The Task Force chairman is John Y. Cole; its members are Alan M. Fern, Beverly Gray, Tao-Tai Hsia, Edward Knight, Lucia J. Rather, Lawrence S. Robinson, Norman J. Shaffer, Robert D. Stevens, Elizabeth F. Stroup, and Glen A. Zimmerman. With my guidance, the Task Force will seek counsel and solicit ideas from the Library's staff and will draw on the advice and suggestions of a number of outside groups chosen to represent the Library's constituencies. The Task Force office is Room 310 in the Main Building. I have asked the Task Force to submit a preliminary report not later than September 1, 1976, and its final report not later than January 15, 1977, when the Task Force and its advisory groups will be dissolved.

I will work closely with the Task Force and the Task Force advisory groups. We want and need the ideas and suggestions of the whole staff. An essential part of the job of the Task Force will be to encourage and ensure this participation.

Our Library, with the generous support and the enlightened guidance of the Congress, has flourished during a century and three-quarters. To establish a Congressional Library as a nation's library was itself a bold and democratic New World innovation. Today, in this great Library, we are the heirs of two complementary traditions: the Tradition of Tradition and the Tradition of Change. If, as I confidently expect, we suggest in the review we now undertake, we can set an example of democratic vitality—of how we can draw on the full resources of our past to meet the surprising and exacting demands of the future.

The Indivisible Community

Speech at the 1976 annual conference of the American
Library Association, Chicago, July 22, 1976

*"Our public libraries are on the way to becoming our forgotten
institution," the new Librarian of Congress told an audience of
professional librarians at the 1976 annual conference of the American
Library Association (ALA). Asked to prepare a talk for a special
program marking the centennial of the association, which was
founded in 1876, Boorstin decided to trace the history of the
American public library movement, explain why he thought public
libraries were threatened, and offer his solutions. A basic theme
was that new technologies have created new opportunities for
books and libraries, and he challenged the national television
networks to lead viewers "from the screens into the wider world
of books." His insistence on this idea would lead, three years
later, to the Library of Congress/CBS Television "Read More
About It" book project.*

$\mathcal{T}$HE PUBLIC LIBRARIES in our time are in limbo. In recent
decades they have been in limbo—in two dictionary senses.
First, limbo as we all know is a region or condition of oblivion
or neglect; and it is also an intermediate place or state. Our
public libraries are on the way to becoming our forgotten
institution—a condition which has come about during the
last few decades—despite the valiant efforts of my predecessors
in the Library of Congress, despite the admirable corporate
work of this association, and despite the personal talents and
energy of all of you.

I will try to suggest some of the historical explanation for
the present situation. I would offer, as a couple of pieces of
evidence, first, some of the observations and pictures in that

delightful book by ALA's Art Plotnik. I am sure many of you have read *Library Life—American Style*, just published last year. The frontispiece, as you will recall, shows the attractive children's librarian for San Mateo County, California, helping two young Californians test the paper birds that they had made in the origami class at the El Granada branch. This suggests the remarkably novel outreach of the roles of libraries in our time. And another clue which might seem less obvious, but which I found rather shocking, is to be found in the *Historical Statistics of the United States* (Bicentennial Edition), which has just been published in two volumes by the Bureau of the Census of the United States Department of Commerce.

In these volumes you will find figures on all sorts of institutions and activities, including the sponge sales in Tarpon Springs, Florida, between 1913 and 1970, but you will not find statistics on libraries. Librarians are listed as part of the labor force, which I suppose is meant to be compliment. And the only aspect of library budgets mentioned is that of the library budgets of institutions of higher learning. There are no statistics on libraries in general nor on public libraries. The last time that the *Historical Statistics of the United States* has such figures was in the 1949 edition.

Here are two clues to what I mean when I say our public libraries are in limbo. Our public libraries have moved into novel, intermediate roles, and they have come to suffer from oblivion or neglect. The situation is very different from that when this association was founded almost one hundred years ago—in early October in Philadelphia at the Centennial Exposition of 1876.

The founding of this association marked what I would call the first heyday of American libraries. The great American library movement took its momentum from three founding principles. The great motive desires in those days were: first, self-help; second, autonomy of the individual; and third, community. These are three of the great founding principles of American civilization.

I would like briefly to suggest how these principles served

the library movement and fulfilled the library movement and then, how the tendencies of history and the drift and momentum of technology have tended to blur or hinder these principles. The great forces at work—and which I will describe—are those which have made ours the Age of Broadcasting.

During the age when the American Library Association came into being there was a great enthusiasm for libraries. It was an age dominated by a democratic ideal, the ideal of spreading knowledge to all. It began, of course, in this country with the celebrated founding of the Boston Public Library in 1854, but that enthusiasm was worldwide. It had been expressed in the Ewart Act in England in 1850 and was articulated in the eloquence of all the great literary figures of the time. Charles Dickens, for example, at the epochal opening of the new library in Manchester, in 1852, called the library "a great free school, bent on carrying instruction to the poorest hearths." When William Makepeace Thackeray, also present on that occasion, saw ahead (in his own words) "the vista of popular libraries being established all over the country, and the educational and elevating influences which would necessarily flow from the extension of the movement," he was so overcome by emotion at that prospect that he had to sit down in the middle of his speech.

In the United States about 1875 there were some 188 public libraries in eleven states. By the turn of the century, the accomplishments of the library movement justified President Theodore Roosevelt's familiar observation (in his annual message to Congress, December 3, 1901) that the modern public library movement was "the most characteristic educational movement of the past fifty years." On that occasion he also described the Library of Congress as "the one National Library in the United States . . . housed in a building which is the largest and most magnificent yet erected for library uses." President Roosevelt said he hoped that the resources to be provided by Congress would enable the Library of Congress "to become not merely a center of research, but the chief

factor in great cooperative efforts for the diffusion of knowledge and the advancement of learning."

I will remind you of some other signs of the prosperity and
enthusiasms and energy of the library movement in those
early years of the American Library Association. In 1870 the
Library of Congress had become a copyright deposit library.
In 1876 appeared the first edition of Dewey's classification
system. We sometimes forget that Melvil Dewey made his
great invention when he was only twenty-five years old. But
we must not let his precocity discourage any of us. In 1887
Melvil Dewey founded his School of Library Economy at
Columbia, where he took the then-bold step of admitting
women.

Between 1874 and 1882 Charles Ammi Cutter's catalog of
the Library of the Boston Athenaeum appeared, providing an
elementary treatise in a pioneer area. From 1886 to 1919 the
great Carnegie gifts were made which came to $40 million
for 1,679 public libraries in 1,412 communities. These gifts
were probably the most economical and productive educational expenditures in all American history.

The Library of Congress played a leading role in this grand
movement. In 1897 the Library of Congress classification
system was developed. In 1901 Herbert Putnam began selling
library cards. These became a national—even an international—symbol of librarians' solidarity. Today, in our world
where nations seem able to agree on almost nothing else, it
remains a cheering omen that they do seem to be able to
agree upon the size of library cards—and the width of motion
picture film. Of course, the Library of Congress had a great
deal to do with creating that symbol.

That was an age of library enthusiasms. If you will look at
any dictionary of quotations of the period, you will be
impressed by the fact that there was hardly a great wit or a
pundit of the age who didn't have something complimentary
and high flown to say about libraries. The most famous of
them perhaps was Thomas Carlyle's observation that "the
true university of these days is a collection of books."

It was part of the general enthusiasm for spreading knowledge. It was part of the reform movement. We forget how widespread were its expressions. If you will read some of the correspondence between the applicants for Carnegie buildings and the Carnegie Foundation, and especially with John Bartram, the man who answered the correspondence for Andrew Carnegie, you will be shocked to see that the money was not awarded for a "building," but for a "bilding." Andrew Carnegie was an enthusiast for spelling reform. So, too, was Melvil Dewey, who also was an enthusiast for the metric system. And these are minor clues to the reformist spirit of the age.

In 1894, when Charles Ammi Cutter ended his first career at the Boston Athenaeum, he went to Northampton, Massachusetts, and made a new career of developing the Forbes Library. In a pioneer manifesto, he said that his hope there would be to shape "a new type of public library, which, speaking broadly, will lend everything to anybody in any desired quantity for any desired time." This was the product of his decades of experience as a pioneering librarian.

Generally speaking, public funds and government support did not match popular enthusiasm. The Library of Congress was an exception. For the Library of Congress has always been blessed by practical purposes. The universal benefits of these emphatically practical—legislative—purposes are not always universally understood in the library profession. We are, as our name wholesomely reminds us, the Library of *Congress*. One of the great features of our Library of Congress is that it has been a branch of congressional good housekeeping. And we hope, of course, that it will remain effective both as the Congress's library and as the nation's library.

There were land grant colleges and there were land grant universities, but—and this is something that we don't see often enough observed—there were no land grant libraries. Of course many library institutions benefited indirectly from the founding of universities—and there were a few men of exceptional vision who gave fortunes for the express and primary purpose of founding libraries. We still profit from their beneficence at the Newberry Library in Chicago and the Huntington Library in San Marino, and there are others. But the great age of college founding (made possible by the fortunes of a Matthew Vassar, a Johns Hopkins, a Leland Stanford, and a John D. Rockefeller) was not matched by a great age of endowed library founding.

It is worth noting, incidentally, that the G.I. Bill after World War II, which brought millions in tuition fees to colleges and universities, gave no comparable direct support to libraries.

The limbo in which public libraries were to find themselves was to be explained also in part by certain traditional peculiarities of the library—and especially the American library—as an institution. I would like to remind you of these briefly.

First, there were conflicts of purpose. The first conflict was between the motive of preservation and the motive of diffusion. The problem was summed up in a statement by one of Bodley's early librarians, who observed that it was his job to protect the books from the public. But many people observed the cemetery-like quality of libraries and some cynics were fond of referring to libraries as places where ideas die. The popular preacher Henry Ward Beecher called the library "the soul's burial ground . . . the land of shadows." Macaulay, in his essay on Milton, you may recall, referred to "the dust and silence of the upper shelf."

In the early public libraries, too, there was much concern over the demeanor and dress of users. "The laboring classes" were thought to be people who might soil the books—and who were unlikely to show books the respect that they were entitled to. This created a conflict between the purpose of diffusion and the purpose of preservation.

There was another conflict of purpose. That was the conflict between the purpose of instruction, or uplift, and the purpose of entertainment. It was embodied in the dispute which I'm sure many of you know, between George Ticknor and his colleague Edward Everett over the proper kinds of books to be included in the Boston Public Library. How popular should the books be? Would you corrupt the taste of young men and women if you let them read books just for entertainment?

This particular conflict was symbolized in the contradictory kinds of appeals that went to Andrew Carnegie in asking for his benefaction. The officers of the Commercial Club in Bloomfield, Iowa, in 1911 appealed for a Carnegie gift for a public library because, they said, they were such a virtuous town. The town had not had a single saloon in thirty years. On the other hand, the mayor of Berlin, Wisconsin, in 1902 argued that their town ought to have a pubic library—in fact needed one more than most others—because in that town there were more than twenty saloons, and there was not one place where a young man could spend his evenings away from the influence of liquor.

This, of course, remains an issue: between uplift or instruction on the one hand and entertainment on the other. It is an issue that becomes increasingly blurred in our Age of Broadcasting.

Another problem of libraries has been that they have tended to be indirect or secondary service institutions. Our Library of Congress is a good example. The Library of Congress was founded primarily in the first instance to serve the Congress, and to help the Congress make more enlightened legislation. For many years the community as a whole was to be benefited by the library only through the improved quality of the works of the lawmakers. The best colonial libraries that were not in the hands of private individuals were also secondary in their services to the general public. The great Harvard College library, for example, was intended to serve the whole community, but only through its service to the select few fortunate enough to be students or faculty at Harvard. The *Historical Statistics of the United States* (Bicentennial Edition) which I mentioned earlier and which offers figures not on public libraries but on the libraries of colleges and universities bears witness to an enduring, misleading, emphasis on libraries as secondary services. Libraries are commonly considered to be institutions designed to serve some other institution.

Nowadays, we find this dramatized in a new way. Our preoccupation with the decay of cities and with multiplying urban problems has tempted politicians—and even "concerned citizens"—to treat public libraries as simply another "municipal service." Like the water supply, the garbage collection arrangements, or the sewerage system, a public library "system" is thought of not as serving people, but as serving "municipalities."

All this has tended to confuse and to bury the identity of the public library. Which has produced another too little-noticed problem. Libraries do not have organized alumni. It is, of course, debatable whether this is entirely a disadvantage, whether it would be an advantage to us to have a football team of the New York Public Library playing against the Detroit Public Library. But, at the same time, our libraries have suffered and lagged behind other educational and public institutions, and partly for this reason. The history of colleges and universities shows how many of their benefactions have come from grateful and also, sometimes, sentimental alumni.

Where are the library alumni? They're everywhere. And they include some of the most successful, most prosperous, and most public-spirited citizens. But the nature of the public library has left them anonymous, invisible, and unenlisted. We don't find people wearing rings certifying that they are a graduate of the Cleveland Public Library. Nor do they attend reunions to increase their hilarity and their devotion.

Students of American history are familiar with Sibley's classic fourteen-volume *Biographical Sketches of Those Who Attended Harvard College*, with Dexter's six volumes on Yale graduates, and with similar works on every major college or university—which all celebrate and advertise their educational achievement. But we have no comparable works on the "graduates" of our great libraries!

Self-made men or men "self-made" with the aid of public libraries, when successful, tend to give their fortunes to colleges and universities. There are some exceptions, but they are relatively few. Libraries generally receive only the crumbs.

And this, too, helps us understand why libraries have been in limbo. They lack an impressive and vivid and familiar corporate identity. While people think of a college as an institution, they tend to think of a public library as a building.

We can, I think, revive the spirit and the motives of the founding era. We can bring our libraries out of limbo, if we will recall the importance of those three principled motives which I mentioned a few minutes ago—self-help, autonomy, and community—and if we succeed in finding special ways to fulfill those purposes in our time.

Now we live in a new era. It is the age not of democratizing knowledge, but the age of democratizing experience. We could sum it up by calling it the Age of Broadcasting.

This Age of Broadcasting is radically different from the previous age, and the novelty can be suggested by the new meaning of the word "broadcast." That word came into our language originally through the usages of agriculture and through Arthur Young's writings on farming. "Broadcast" as an adjective first meant "scattered abroad"—that is, scattered over the whole surface of the soil instead of being sowed in drills or rows.

"Broadcast" entered our language in a new sense in 1922 when radio made it possible to scatter messages in a new way, without regard to roads or walls; scattered abroad by the wireless telegraphy was the meaning which then came in.

One of the special features, revolutionary features, of this new kind of diffusion was that now messages were to be scattered in a new sense. They were sent out to anonymous, undetermined, even indeterminate, audiences. You might still know who was sending the message but there was a new mystery—who was listening?

How much were they listening to? And how seriously were they listening? This new mystery then created a new science, the science of market research—and a science which has not yet unraveled all of the mystery by any means.

Coincidentally with this and as a result of the same

technology which made it possible to broadcast, it became possible to spread abroad a whole new set of sensations. What was spread about now was not what was spread in the previous Age of Publishing. Technology had changed and enlarged what could be diffused. In this new era what was diffused was not merely the familiar old product—the printed written word or the graven image—not merely the translation of experience by an author or an artist, but the very sensations of experience.

Living sounds. Living voices. Moving living images. In living color. What was diffused was not just knowledge but *experience*. Experience of distant places, great events, people in high stations. What were some of the new consequences of this for the spreading of other kinds of messages—those which we have in our charge?

In the first place, now messages were taken to the people. Formerly, people had to go after the messages. The motive of self-help was partly removed. Now people could simply sit there—at home, or wherever else they happened to be—and get the message.

Second, it became an age of networks and channels. This was to be an age of the decline of choice, the decline of autonomy.

And finally, and this will be most important for us who want to promote the public library movement, it was an age of the decline of community. People now found it less necessary to congregate—to come together in the visible presence of other human beings. Community was attenuated as people were segregated into their own living rooms. The paradox was that there was to be a strange communalizing of experience and vivifying of experience along with this new segregation of individuals.

This democratizing of experience came as the climax of one of the most rapid and most remarkable revolutions in history. We have lived through a cataclysm of technology. And most of this has come in the century since the American Library Association was founded.

It was a coincidence, but there was deep symbolic significance in the fact that the Philadelphia exposition of 1876, the occasion when the American Library Association was founded, was also the first grand national exhibit of the marvels of technology. That was the occasion of the successful demonstration of Alexander Graham Bell's telephone, which was itself a clue to the electronic roots of many new problems. The technological momentum of the new age was signaled by the development of the phonograph, built by Thomas A. Edison in 1877, by the incandescent lamp which he made commercially practicable in 1879, and by the rise of the photograph, which was announced when the first popular camera was patented by George Eastman under the name of Kodak in 1888. Celluloid, which proved essential to the development of movies, was patented by Edison in 1888. Radio came by 1920 when David Sarnoff was marketing his radio music boxes.

And then of course, the climax—television— whose arrival in our time I remember vividly. The first commercial TV broadcasting stations appeared in the United States in 1941, when there were two. Seven years later, in 1948, there were 108 stations and a million sets. By 1970 over 95 percent of American households had television.

The consequences of this in democratizing experience were overwhelming. The result—so commonplace that we do not even realize it—has been to change the very nature of time and space. Now you're more there when you're here than when you're there.

The tendency of this Age of Broadcasting, moreover, is to broadcast everything. Even the mails—that formerly were a means of complimenting people by addressing messages to them personally—became addressed to that universal, anonymous, irritating destination "Occupant." Junk mail is nothing but broadcasting by nonelectronic means. It is a way of spreading something abroad without regard to whether the person who receives it wants it or needs it.

Even book publishing, increasingly dominated by the market for paperbacks, has tended to become a kind of broadcasting. Paperback books are marketed by being "scattered over the whole surface" of the market. They are not destined for particular purchasers but spread abroad in the hope that somebody—anybody—will pick them up. As paperback publishers remind us, perhaps the most important feature of a paperback is the jacket design. Paperbacks are marketed on newsstands and in airport kiosks where they compete with magazines, candy bars, and other items bought on impulse. One of the most successful publishers of paperback books reports that items that have not already shown their impulse appeal in these markets are expected to be returned after nine days.

Libraries, we hope, can provide us an escape from the limitations of this broadcast world. But here we must be wary of falling into a common fallacy in the interpretation of history. This is what I call the Displacive Fallacy.

We are tempted to think—and this may be due in part to our excessive faith in technology—that, just as a victorious army defeats its enemies, so the new technology conquers the old technology. It is easy to find examples of mistaken prophecies based on the Displacive Fallacy. For example, there were confident predictions that the telephone would abolish the mail. There were firm predictions that the radio would make the telephone obsolete. That the phonograph would be the end of live concerts. That television would be the end of radio. Then, of course, that television would abolish the book. And now, that the computer will displace humankind.

All these predictions were based on a misconception. Shall we say a teleological misconception? A misconception about the purpose or end for which people invent technology and develop their institutions. It is a misconception which is quite un-American. For it rests on the notion that technology is simply a way to satisfy fixed needs. If you satisfy the needs in one way, then you won't have to satisfy them in another way. The history of technology and of institutions is not, however, the story of "instead." It is the story of "also."

Experience is not substitutive, but additive and cumulative. The American experience—the very existence of American experience, on this, the most unnecessary of all continents— proved that human needs and wants can be ever-expanding. The great inventors do not merely satisfy needs, they invent needs. This is what I call the Exploring Spirit, which I describe in my little volume of that title (Random House, 1976).

Printed books were among the first great stirrers of the Exploring Spirit. They created and awakened a vast range of unimagined wants and needs. Who wanted an automobile? What people wanted was a better horse or a better carriage. Henry Ford not only invented a new means of transportation; it would be most misleading to put it that way. He invented a new need. The automobile. Then came television. And now, of course, the computer, which reaches farther out beyond the imagined needs of scholars than any of its predecessors.

The new technology, then, has not abolished libraries or the book and never will. But it has created new roles for books and for libraries. Libraries can provide escapes from the new limitations of our Age of Broadcasting. First, I will suggest some of the new opportunities that our age has provided for the book and for libraries. These arise out of the very peculiarities of our novel ways of democratizing experience. Then I will suggest some of the ways in which we as librarians may make wider and more effective use of the characteristic products of the Age of Broadcasting toward our more traditional purposes.

In the first place, the library has a new opportunity to promote the motive and the desire for self-help. It is an antidote for the declining sense of skill. The TV audience is skill-less and only half-attentive. TV-land, a supremely democratic land where all can enter free of charge, is a world where no skill is required as a passport. There are few levels of TV-viewing. Anybody can get something from watching a tennis match or "All in the Family." Only a few can get anything from reading Kant or Proust or Joyce. While reading is graded, television-viewing can only be restricted. What is

X-rated is not so rated because it's hard to understand, but because it's too easy to understand.

In the world of books, by contrast, you skill increases your reach. Printing, once called the *ars artium omnium conservatrix*, might now also be called the art stimulative of all the arts.

Now libraries are needed as the antidote to the undifferentiated audience—and to preserve the motive of autonomy by encouraging the individual and conserving the small group with a specialized interest. Television has a congenital emphasis on entertainment, because entertainment is an activity with the most undifferentiated appeals. "Educational television" nowadays is presented as if it were some startling innovation. But there have been educational books for centuries.

The book has long since offered in high degree the special individualized virtues of cable television. Every book ultimately is aimed at an audience of one. A book can be published without even being assigned a channel. The publisher need not produce any certain amount of religious matter, need not advertise the community activities. He can even suggest the benefits of smoking or of any activity which is beginning to be unrespectable in the community as a whole. Libraries, moreover, are a natural antidote everywhere to the perils of the government-controlled broadcasting channel. We librarians are the natural conservers and promoters of free communication.

While publishing in the United States has moved farther and farther away from censorship, broadcasting even in our free country has come increasingly under government scrutiny, and is likely to become ever more so. As TV-land finds it ever harder to be, the world of the book is the land of the free and the home of the brave.

The library is an antidote—ever more needed in the Age of Broadcasting—to patron control. While we think of television as our most modern medium, in one crucial respect television has stayed back in the eighteenth century. About that time the book began to escape from the dominance of rich and powerful patrons. But broadcasting still remains in the Age of the Patron.

The broadcasting audience can respond only indirectly to what the patron provides on the airwaves—by buying or not buying the product. In the world of the book, however, the reader and the buyer remain sovereign.

Finally, the library can be an avenue into the whole human community. It can be a corrective to TV-myopia—the myopia which enlarges out of all proportion our sense of the contemporary, which widens and shortens our vision of the chronological foreground. That myopia makes it difficult for us to see what extends back beyond the age of photography.

The great electronic conqueror of space cannot conquer time. Only the book—and the other media that we have at our disposal—can accomplish that. Books remain our messengers from the longer past and to the longer future.

Books remain, and libraries remain, our symbols of community with all humankind. With the worldwide rise and multiplication of chauvinisms, the library and the book remain our escape from the prison of the present and from the provincialism of our nation's confines.

These are some of the ways in which the peculiar limitations of broadcasting have given new roles to books and to libraries. But the new technology of the Age of Broadcasting itself offers us new opportunities. In conclusion I will briefly suggest some of these.

Radio and television are not enemies of the book. They can be new allies of the book. We must recognize and enlist our new allies. They can help us in our mission of the diffusion of knowledge and the advancement of learning. We must find ways to make television our ally, to make it the trailer and the appetizer for the library and the whole world of books.

Television channels, which must justify themselves for their public service, announce freely and frequently the time, the weather, the news, the latest catastrophe, and the next television program (which sometimes ought to be classified in that category). It's astonishing—it's even shocking—to me that our conscience-flaunting television networks have taken so little responsibility for leading viewers from the television screens into the wider world of books that is always waiting. We, as book people and as librarians, must see that that's changed. Of course, we occasionally see the announcement of the names of printed matter and books in book-review programs and book-discussion programs. But these are generally aimed at small audiences and seldom appear on the commercial networks. Generally when we see a book listed, it is in the credits for a television program. When we are simply told the name of a book that a program has been adapted from, we often conclude that now we needn't bother to read to the book, since we've seen the television program instead.

But that situation need not remain. Recently at a convention of the Association of American Publishers, I suggested that we seek new ways to use television to make TV-viewers into more avid book readers and more enthusiastic library users. The book publishers, who are already undertaking an imaginative program to use television during the coming Christmas season to persuade more TV-viewers to become book buyers, greeted my suggestion with enthusiasm. They will cooperate in our efforts as librarians to improve the reading habits and widen and deepen the literacy of our nation of TV audiences. We have a hint of how far we still have to go, and how much persuading we still need to do, in the fact that the leading "cultural" correspondent of our leading national newspaper snidely reported my suggestion as the kind of thinking that had brought the dinosaur to his doom. But we must and can and will find ways to enlarge contemporary literacy. We will use the television screen itself to alert people to the wealth that awaits them in libraries and the whole world of books.

We must find ways, moreover, to give to our library users wider choices not only in the world of books, but in all the other means of democratizing experience. Of course, most of our libraries are already offering these choices, but we should do even more—to offer the increasing product of sound and sight recording.

We must find ways to use our technology (certainly the computer, but not only the computer) to help us develop networks which will enable us to share our resources. All this will help us accomplish the purpose which Josiah Quincy described in 1841 (the hope of those who were trying to found a Boston Public Library), "to give the intellectual treasures of the civilized world the same dissemination and equalization which commerce [had] already given to its material ones."

Just as the Library of Congress, inspired by that great librarian Herbert Putnam, has advanced in the past three-quarters of a century from the centrally prepared library card and interlibrary loans into countless other ways of sharing, so now the computer can open a new era of collaboration and shared resources. The computer enables us in new and starling ways to repeal the traditional laws of physics, which once declared that anything can be in only one place at a time.

The Age of Broadcasting calls for a library renaissance. There is an unprecedented need for the unique resources of the book. At the same time there are crushing new pressures which disintegrate and discourage the grand improving motives of self-help, autonomy, and community. But there are vast new resources which we can use to nourish these very motives, to encourage them, and to give them a justified sense of fulfillment. Libraries remain the meccas of self-help. They remain as they have always been, the most open of open universities—institutions of the highest learning, where there are no entrance examinations, no registration fees, no examinations, and no diplomas, and where one can enter at any age. There we make available the great teachers of all ages and all nations. We have no problem with tenure. In this invisible endless faculty of great teachers, they all have tenure, and yet none of them becomes senile or lazy, nor can they inhibit their successors. And we need not worry that any of them will be distracted from their teaching.

We have no problems there of "publish or perish," for there the published never perishes. As librarians we share the mission of the greatest teachers: To help others help themselves. This is what we mean by autonomy, independence, self-government—the ideals of a democratic people. Libraries remain islands of choice in a world of channels.

In this supermarket of ideas and arts, every citizen can choose his nourishment from the products old and new, of the whole human race. Ours is a workshop of do-it-yourself programming, where no citizen need wait for a national broadcast or even a local station.

The library is par excellence a place of community, for there we share the spiritual wealth of all humankind. We must find ways to enlist the material wealth of our nation—at all levels, federal, state, and local—to accomplish and fulfill this community. In the United States, of all places, our library institutions are products of community, mostly local communities.

We must strengthen our libraries as communities of the Exploring Spirit. Places where people are stirred to ask questions they never imagined from people they never knew. Where people are enticed into the adventures of the unexpected, the unknown, and the unimagined. Where we nourish creative dissatisfaction, where the human hunger for knowledge and the appetite for enlarging experience are stirred in the very act of searching.

We librarians must explore together in our search for new worlds of autonomy, self-help, and community. The Library of Congress pledges its friendly fellowship in this common adventure, an adventure which brings us out of limbo and which will fulfill our special American vision of a community of communities.

To Preserve Civilization

Welcoming Remarks at a Planning Conference for a
National Preservation Program, Library of Congress,
December 16, 1976

*As Librarian of Congress, Boorstin frequently was called upon to
open conferences and meetings at the Library. It was a task he
took seriously and performed gracefully. Moreover, his view of a
conference topic (no matter what the topic) invariably broadened
the horizons of the audience and the conference organizers themselves. His opening comments at a conference to begin planning
the Library's national preservation program are a good example.*

WELCOME to the Library of Congress. I think most of you
have been here before. We hope you will come again and
again. Let me try to suggest the large scope of, and our hopes
for, this conference.

We are here to preserve civilization. There is no other way
to describe our concern, and I think that this may even be an
understatement. You may recall the story about Oliver Wendell
Holmes, Jr., who went into his office across the street in the
Supreme Court one fifteenth of March with a smile on his
face, and, when his assistant asked what he was smiling
about, the justice replied, "Why, today I had the pleasure of
paying my income tax and with my taxes I buy civilization."
That kind of view of how you preserve civilization is not
universal, and I think some of us might even doubt whether
increases in taxes are a measure of the progress of civilization.
But I do think that when Frazer Poole and his colleagues go
to their laboratories here in the Library they can without
exaggeration say they are concerned with preserving civilization.

There is no proper definition of civilization that does not include the preservation of printed matter, and one thing that has struck me as Librarian is the general ignorance concerning preservation. Preservation of printed matter is, I think, the great forgotten problem of our age. It has been forgotten, not by specialists and librarians but, to a surprising extent, by scholars, men of affairs, and those who use the materials of civilization.

It is hard even to find a suitable metaphor for this problem. Most of you know much more about it than I do, but I have begun to get a sense of its extent and gravity. The problem is all the more serious because it is so undramatic, because the forces which destroy these materials of civilization leave our houses and buildings and furnishings intact but seem to have a very special appetite for the most important products of modern civilization.

The purpose of this conference is to assess the proportions of the problem, to alert the nation and the world to it, and then to find ways both to deal with it for the present and to minimize it for the future. We already have some conception of the nature and extent of the problem through work done here in the Library and elsewhere in the institutions that you all represent.

But we need to know more; we need to pool our knowledge and our efforts. A conference held here in December 1965 and sponsored by the Association of Research Libraries and the Library of Congress began to explore the issue. Much has been done since then, but the problem is vast. I might just suggest why we find it necessary to bring together both technologists and persons concerned with the social effects of preservation.

The problem, as you know, has two aspects at least. One is technological or physical—that is, it concerns how to deal with the materials, the paper, the ink, and the bindings. Also, however, there is the social, or what I would call the epistemological, problem; it involves the question of the priorities and techniques of selecting what is to be preserved, of distributing the responsibility for those choices, and for organizing the cooperation. The technology is a *sine qua non* and that is something it is well to remind people of, especially in this city and in our location. If you don't know how to perform a task, there's no use organizing for the purpose—although, in Washington and elsewhere, it frequently seems to be assumed that if ignorance is well enough organized and bureaucratized, and is supported by enough votes, somehow the problem of no knowledge will disappear.

Persuasion is not enough. Unfortunately, the physical world (unlike the voting populace or even sometimes the Congress) is not tolerant of our ignorance. If the key doesn't fit, the lock won't be opened. But the technological solutions will not help us unless we have the social solutions. And I hesitate to use the word *solutions*; I perhaps should use *mitigations*.

We must discover the needs and opportunities for collaboration if we are to use effectively the technological solutions. Finally, the social solution becomes the *sine qua non*. The social problem and the technological problem are interrelated. For example, if we could persuade publishers to print books on permanent/durable paper, the problem of preservation for the future would be considerably reduced, and this also would reduce the urgency for finding deep freeze storage or some other device for preservation.

My role then, this morning, is to remind you, and all of us, of the grandeur of our opportunity. If the preservation problem, the brittle books problem, is one of cataclysmic proportions, it does offer us an opportunity of cataclysmic grandeur, to save the record of our civilization, past and future. It is the duty of the Library of Congress to take the leadership in this undertaking—in a collaborative spirit, appropriate to an institution of collaboration, cooperation, and compromise. We must find ways of working together, of using all the knowledge, and the good will, and all the energy and imagination represented in this room and in the nation. This is why, with the generous assistance of the Council on Library Resources, we have called this conference.

We ask for all of your suggestions and help, not only today and tomorrow, but when you go home. With your assistance, we intend to develop, and we will develop here at the Library of Congress, a program of national preservation. The termites of "brittledom" eat away even while we talk here today and tomorrow, and their taste for modernity plagues us increasingly. We need your help and cooperation. Drawing on the suggestions you offer here, we will undertake a program which we hope will eventually become adequate to the gargantuan and enticing proportions of the problem.

A Historian to the Librarians

Address to the Annual Conference of the International Federation of Library Associations, Brussels, Belgium, September 5, 1977

Boorstin's speech to participants at the 1977 annual conference of the International Federation of Library Associations addressed important, recurrent themes such as the book as a triumph of human technology and the Displacive Fallacy, which assumes that each new technology displaces (rather than transforms) the preceding technology. Speaking as a historian, Boorstin also discussed the role of the librarian in the new technological age.

I<small>T</small> is a great pleasure to be here today and especially to share the platform with a cosmonaut. But, while I applaud his sentiments, I should remind you that in some respects he has a much easier job than has been assigned to me. He speaks for the cosmonauts who, unfortunately, are still a small community. I have been asked to speak for historians, who not only are a large and varied community but have a special mission which should make you suspicious of anyone who pretends to speak for historians. A historian is by definition a person who encourages and helps other to speak for themselves, and who therefore should only speak for himself.

Ever since there have been historians, the library has been the historian's natural habitat. Librarians have kept house for us, you have nourished us. Although we have been sometimes impatient with you, you have been wonderfully patient with us. You have helped us ask the unasked question and have helped us try to answer the unanswerable. We—historians and librarians—have lived so long and so intimately together that it would be superfluous, if not embarrassing (and out of tune with the spirit of the age) at this late date to try to regularize the relationship with a formal marriage.

But in the late twentieth century there are some special reasons for continuing or even increasing our intimacy. There are many things which librarians can do for historians which historians may not be willing or able to do for themselves.

The role that I am suggesting is not merely one of symbiosis (which the dictionary defines as "the relationship of two different organisms in a close association that may not necessarily be of benefit to each"). The long confidential relationship between us qualifies the librarian to guide us historians, to save us both from our own weaknesses and from our own and our society's peculiar successes.

The new technology of communication in the United States—television and radio, reinforced by the daily press—has begun to afflict us with a new myopia. This is a chronological myopia, a short-sightedness. Our vision and our consciousness are filled with the recent and the present. Today's trivia from the other side of the world crowd out of our consciousness the grand world-shaking life-shaping events of earlier centuries. Television takes us across the oceans and the continents, even into outer space, and overwhelms us with eyewitness news. It can cross the world but it cannot cross the centuries.

The Book remains our main, in many respects our only vehicle across those centuries. The Book, although we sometimes forget it, is itself one of the great triumphs of human technology. The librarian has long served as our chronological cosmonaut, our guide into the adventurous, dangerous dimensions of outer time.

Now, willy nilly, the librarian is caught in a maelstrom of technological change. Within the last century, and especially within the last five decades, the book has acquired more competitors than it had acquired in all the previous five centuries. As historians and as librarians it is our duty to find our bearings in these multiform records of human experience, and to help others get their bearings.

In high-technology societies, like the United States, our enthusiasm for the new leads us to what I call the Displacive Fallacy. This is the belief that a new technology displaces the old, and drives it from the field as a conquering army disperses the enemy. Pundits not so long ago prophesied that the telephone would displace the mails, that radio would displace the telephone, that the phonograph would displace live orchestras, and of course, that television would substantially displace both radio and the book. In the library world only a few decades ago some microfilm enthusiasts were predicting that microforms would displace books. Now we hear similar predictions of how audiovisual aids, motion pictures, tape recordings, television, or the computer will displace the book— or perhaps human beings themselves.

Despite some conspicuous exceptions, the general rule in history is that a new technology does not displace but rather transforms or finds new uses for an earlier technology. Printing did not make handwriting obsolete. The automobile has not displaced the bicycle. Television has not displaced the telephone or radio.

The Displacive Fallacy, however, assumes that there are only a limited number of social functions and that the categories of experience are not expandable. Such a static view is quite uncongenial to my pragmatic, experimental, and somewhat American way of thinking. Experience is ever expanding. New inventions do not simply fill old needs, for the inventor himself concocts new needs. He actually invents new forms of experience. Nobody "needed" the telephone, radio, or television. They were not the product of widespread demand but actually added new dimensions to human experience and created new demands.

This simple fact has momentous implications both for the historian and the librarian. For each new technology produces its own new kind of record and leaves its own special new residue. If the historian is to chronicle the full range of human experience he must find ways to use, and must find the meaning of using, them all. The librarian has a special responsibility to save us from the Displacive Fallacy.

More than that. The librarian now has the responsibility to us all, but perhaps especially to the historian, to be a mediator among the media. The advocates and marketers of the several technologies are partisan competitors. The librarian must make them complementary sources of knowledge and of experience. With every new technology the whole kaleidoscope of life is given a twist. Everything has its new place in the new pattern. The librarian can help us discover that pattern.

The modern librarian should of course be a lover and champion of the book. But he cannot be bookish. He must be alert to see how every new technology illuminates its predecessor—and those that follow. What can we historians learn from the photograph or the phonograph record or the map or the motion picture film or the tape recording or radio or television that we cannot learn from the book? Or from the book that we cannot learn from them? Librarians help us turn the kaleidoscope of experience, help us see, enjoy, and learn from the new design.

Librarians, too, have the special opportunity to help us escape from the increasing centralization of education and the increasing power of increasingly centralized forms of communication, such as radio and television. These forms of *wholesale* communication—school curricula, radio and television programs—are bureaucratically controlled, and difficult to change. For example, if we in the United States want to redress the imbalance of our American liberal education and awaken our citizens to all human history (not just the Christian, or the Western-European-American history) by introducing them to the cultures of Africa, the cultures of Islam, the civilizations of the Middle East, of India, China, and Japan, we have a most difficult task. The academic ruts, even in the United States, are deep and hard to get out of.

The book, however, is preeminently a form of *retail* communication. When the book matters, it is always in the last analysis directed to an audience of one. Our librarians have the power to cosmopolitanize our thinking, to open individual windows for individual readers whom they can interest, opening out on the grand vistas of the civilizations that have otherwise been given no proper place in our history. The special power of librarians comes especially from the fact that they are dealing with the individual book, the individual reader. The library is happily a place where the rivulets of freedom, of heterodoxy, of ingenuity, and of genius can freely flow. No government has yet discovered a successful way of enforcing birth control over ideas. The private thinker reading a book of his choice is beyond the reach to tyrants. Librarians, precisely because they are *not* teaching from a curriculum, are freer to be guides to help learners find their own way.

We librarians and historians share this mission of enlarging the human consciousness. We are the De-provincializers, the Cosmopolitanizers of all parts of the human race. The historian enriches our understanding of man and civilization with his unique perspective of a part of the world's past from some part of the world's present. But the librarian has a larger, less idiosyncratic, role. He is a guide and a therapist. He can help save us wherever we are from our special provincialisms—of our profession, of our nation, of our generation, of our politics, of our technology. He can lead us into the dark continents of knowledge, into the unexplored wildernesses of questions we never thought of asking.

The librarian's unique role is as the public accountant of our intellectual life. He can insist that we keep the full record, not neglecting either the debits or the credits. He can remind us of our failures and our deficiencies, of the gaps in our record and our knowledge of ourselves and of others. He can help save us from the accidents of our birth—so that we become in our thoughts not mere citizens of the late twentieth century or of the United States or some other country, but witnesses of all past generations, citizens of the whole indivisible world.

A Center for the Book in the Library of Congress

Remarks at the first meeting of the National Advisory
Board for the Center for the Book, Library of Congress,
October 20, 1977

*No theme was more dominant in Librarian Boorstin's earliest
statements than the need to keep alive the Tradition of the Book.
This concept, endorsed by his Task Force on Goals, Organization,
and Planning, led to the creation of the Center for the Book in
the Library of Congress. Established by Public Law 95-129,
approved October 13, 1977, the center was to be a partnership
between the Library and the private sector, which would support
its projects and programs. Anticipating passage of the law, early
in October the Librarian began inviting members of the private
sector from around the country to attend the first meeting of the
center's National Advisory Board, which was held one week after
the new law had been approved.*

*Y*ou may wonder why the Library of Congress, which, of
all places on earth, is a center for the book, should now
become a place for the establishing of *the* Center for the Book.
It is to organize, focus, and dramatize our nation's interest
and attention on the book, to marshal the nation's support,
spiritual, physical, and fiscal, for the book.

The Times call for it. Why? Because this is a multimedia,
electronic, media-ridden, annual model age.

The Place is here. This institution has a greater vested
interest in the book than any other place on earth. For us, the
book is not only a vested interest but a vested idea. Because
we at the Library of Congress collect knowledge and enter-

tainment resources in all media—in film and on tape, on phonograph records and on motion pictures, in manuscript, from radio and television, on maps—as well as in books, and we have the world's great collections in these media; because we are the greatest copyright deposit in all formats; because we collect in all languages (468 at the last count!); because we have been doing this for 177 years, and will go on for more centuries. Because of all this, we know, better than anyone else, the dangers of the book being stifled, drowned, suffocated, buried, obscured, mislaid, misunderstood, ununderstood, unread—both from neglect and from the rising level of the increasing flood. Because we do serve the Congress, whose interests know no bounds, because we serve all libraries, scholars of all sorts and conditions, teachers, readers, quasi-readers, semi-readers, and even, we suspect, nonreaders. As the national library of a great free republic, we have a special duty and a special interest to see that books *do not* go unread, that they *are* read by people of all ages and conditions, that books are not buried in their own excess, under their own dross, not lost from neglect or obscured from us by specious alternatives and synthetic substitutes. As the national library of the most technologically advanced nation on earth, we have a special duty, too, to see that the book is the useful, illuminating servant of all other technologies, and that all other technologies become the effective, illuminating acolytes of the book.

The Library of Congress is our mission headquarters, but we hope and expect to train and encourage missionaries all over our nation. Unlike some other missions, this mission is explosively ecumenical. No other mission can be more ecumenical. For the book is the most conservative and the most liberal, the most traditional and the most revolutionary of media, the most atheistical and the most reverential, the most retrospective and the most futuristic. It is our duty to keep that mission energetically alive. The book is the reservoir of all the ideas that we have forgotten, and it will be the reservoir for ideas still unborn.

Today we are here, encouraged by our Congress and our President, hosted by the greatest library on earth, to find ways to fill the special needs of our time and our nation, to seize the opportunities I have suggested, to find new opportunities, and to keep ourselves ready for still new opportunities. Here we make plans for a grand national effort to make all our people eager, avid, understanding, critical readers. To make this age, this nation, and this place the staging ground for a Renaissance of the Book.

Gresham's Law: Knowledge or Information?

Remarks at the White House Conference on Library
and Information Services, Washington,
November 19, 1979

*Boorstin's remarks at the White House Conference were probably
quoted and reprinted more than any other statement he made while
Librarian of Congress. Emphasizing the distinction between information and knowledge, he decried the conditions which permit
society's knowledge-institutions, which include its libraries, to "go
begging." He felt that extravagant or misplaced expectations "for
the role of information or the devices which serve it" could lead
to the isolation of the world of scholarship from the world of
libraries. Within the Library of Congress two new entities were
created to help avoid such dangers: the Center for the Book and
the Council of Scholars.*

$\mathcal{A}$S THE LIBRARIAN OF CONGRESS I speak for a national fortress
of knowledge. In other words, I speak for a library, and for
libraries. Our relentless Jeffersonian quest tempts us to believe
that all technologies (and perhaps, too, all ideas) are created
equal. This favored axiom is only slightly clouded by another
axiom, equally American. For we have a touching national
belief in annual models. In our national lexicon, "newer" is
a synonym for "better." The result is illustrated in the title—
and I suspect, too, in the preoccupations—of this conference.
Libraries (or as you say "library services") are here equated
with "information services," which is perilously close to saying
that knowledge can or should be equated with information.

In these remarks I would like to focus your attention on
the distinction between knowledge and information, the

importance of the distinction, and the dangers of failing to recognize it. You have a hint of my theme in the melodramatic difference today between the condition of our knowledge-institutions and our information-institutions. The last two decades have seen the spectacular growth of the information industry. We are exhilarated by this example of American ingenuity and enterprise—the frontier spirit in the late twentieth century. A magic computer technology now accomplishes the dreariest tasks in seconds, surpasses the accuracy of the human brain, controls production lines and refineries, arranges inventories, and retrieves records. All this makes us proud of the human imagination.

All this, too, I am glad to say, has produced a widening unpredicted world of profit and employment. The information industry, we are happy to note, is flourishing. It is a growth industry. It enjoys the accelerating momentum of technology and the full vitality of the marketplace. The information industries are a whole new world of business celebrity. The jargon of the stock exchange accurately describes theirs as "glamour" stocks. Their leaders hold the national spotlight, and with good reason. The President of the United States appoints the head of one of the greatest of these companies to be perhaps our most important ambassador—to the Soviet Union.

Meanwhile, what has become of our knowledge-institutions? They do not deal mainly in the storage and retrieval of information, nor in the instant flow of today's facts and figures which will be displaced by tomorrow's reports and bulletins. Rather, they deal in the enduring treasure of our whole human past. They include our colleges and our universities—and, of course, our libraries. While the information industry flourishes and seeks new avenues of growth, while people compete to buy into them, our knowledge-institutions go begging.

Knowledge-institutions do not pay the kind of dividends that are reflected on the stock market. They are sometimes called "philanthropic," which means that they profit nobody except everybody and their dividends go to the whole community. These knowledge-institutions—and especially our public libraries—ask charity, the community's small change, just to keep their heat and their lights on, and to keep their unrenovated doors open. We, the knowledge-institutions, are the poor relations. We anxiously solicit, and gratefully acknowledge, the crumbs. Today I would like to put into historical perspective the distinction between knowledge and information. For it is especially appropriate in this White House Conference that we should focus on the distinction.

In my lifetime we have moved from an Age of Publishing into our Age of Broadcasting. In that Age of Publishing started by Gutenberg, printed materials (bearing the community's memory, wisdom, literary imagination, and knowledge) were, of course, widely diffused. The great vehicle was the book. Knowledge was thought to be cumulative. The new books did not displace the old. When today's books arrived people did not throw away yesterday's—as if they were newspapers or out-of-date information bulletins. On the contrary, the passing years gave a new vitality to the books of past centuries.

We too easily forget that the printed book, too, was a triumph of technology. The dead could now speak, not only to the select few who could afford a manuscript book but to thousands at home, in schools, and in libraries everywhere. The very words of Homer, Plato, Machiavelli, and Dickens now could reach everybody. Books became the carriers and the record—also the catalyst and the incentive—for most of the knowledge, the amusement, and the sacred visions of the human race. The printed book has given all humanity its inexpensive, speedy, reliable vehicles across the centuries. Books have conquered time.

But the peculiar, magic vehicles of our age conquer space. The tube makes us constant eyewitnesses of riots in Iran, airplane wrecks in India, children starving in Cambodia, and guerrilla attacks in Rhodesia. Along, of course, with an ever-flowing current of entertainment programs. Yet the special commodity of our electronic Age of Broadcasting is *Information*—in all its amplitude, in all its formats.

While knowledge is orderly and cumulative, information is random and miscellaneous. We are flooded by messages from the instant-everywhere in excruciating profusion. In our ironic twentieth-century version of Gresham's law, information tends to drive knowledge out of circulation. The oldest, the established, the cumulative, is displaced by the most recent, the most problematic. The latest information on anything and everything is collected, diffused, received, stored, and retrieved before anyone can discover whether the facts have meaning.

A mountain-climbing syndrome rules us. Information is gathered simply because it is there. Electronic devices for diffusion, storage, and retrieval are used, simply because they too are there. Otherwise, the investment would seem wasted! I am not complaining. On the contrary, I am charmed and amazed. For so much of human progress has come from people playing enthusiastically with their new technologic toys—with results that are astonishing, and often productive.

Whatever the motive, we see the knowledge industry being transformed, and even to some extent displaced, by an information industry. In the schoolroom, history tends to be displaced by current events. The resources of science and literature are overwhelmed and diluted by multiplying journals, by loose-leaf services, by preprints, and by information stored in computers, quickly and conveniently modified, and instantly retrievable.

To the ancient question, "What is truth?" we American now reply, "Sorry, I haven't seen the seven o'clock news!"

What does all this mean for the world of knowledge, which is also, of course, the world of libraries? It should be plainer than ever that our libraries are needed to keep civilization in perspective. The more electronic our society becomes, the more urgent it is that we have prosperous knowledge-institutions. Yet this urgency is less noted every year. If you consult the authoritative *Encyclopedia of the Social Sciences*, published in 1933, and look under "Libraries" you will be referred to "Public Libraries" where you find an extensive article. But if you consult its successor, the *International*

Encyclopedia of the Social Sciences, published in 1968, and look for an entry for "Libraries" you will find no article. Instead there's a cross-reference which says "See under Information and Storage and Retrieval."

The fashionable chronologic myopia of our time tempts enthusiasts to forget the main and proper mission of our libraries. "Libraries have been selling the wrong product for years," one such faddist exclaims. "They have been emphasizing reading. The product that we have is information." But these are false messiahs. Of course, we must use computer technology and enlist the whole information industry. At the Library of Congress we have tried to be a leader in exploring its uses and in extending its applications. We will continue to do so.

In the long run, however, we will serve neither the information industry nor our civilization if we encourage extravagant or misplaced expectations for the role of information or the devices which serve it up. We must never forget that our libraries are our fortresses of knowledge. If we allow these rich resources, still preserved mainly in books, to be displaced by the latest thing, by today's news and journals and preprints and loose-leaf services and telephone conversations and currently revised printouts, we will isolate the world of scholarship from the world of libraries. To avoid such dangers as these we have established in the Library of Congress a Center for the Book, to use old and find new ways to keep the book flourishing, to keep people reading books, and to enlist other media to promote reading. One such project, "Read More About It," with the enthusiastic collaboration of CBS, the other night after the showing of "All Quiet on the Western Front" brought our suggested reading list to some thirty-one million viewers. We must and will do more of this.

If librarians cease to be scholars in order to become computer experts, scholars will cease to feel at home in our libraries. And then our whole citizenry will find that our libraries add little to their view of the world, but merely reinforce the pressures of the imperial instant-everywhere. To enlist scholars more actively and more intimately in the activities of the Library of Congress we are now setting up in the Library a Council of Scholars. They will help us discover the needs of the scholarly world and will help us provide an ongoing inventory of the state of our knowledge—and of our ignorance.

A great civilization needs many and varied resources. In our time our libraries have two paradoxical and sometimes conflicting roles. Of course we must be repositories of information. But somehow we must also remain places of refuge from the tidal waves of information—and misinformation. Our libraries must be conspicuously the treasuries of news that stays news.

The era of the Enlightenment, the later eighteenth century, the age of Franklin and Jefferson, the founding epoch of our nation, was an Age of Publishing. That age has left us a happy phrase. They said that people should read for "*Amusement and Instruction.*" This was why they read the poetry of Dryden and Pope, the philosophy of Hume, the history of Gibbon, and the novels of Sterne and Fielding. The two delights, "amusement" and "instruction," were inseparable. The book was the prototypical provider of both. A person who was "a-mused" (from Latin "muser," to idle or to pass the time) was engaged in a quite autonomous activity—set off by a catalyst, in the form of a book. In those days book publishing was an "amusement industry."

Today in a Age of Broadcasting "entertainment" tends to displace "amusement." While we once had to amuse ourselves, we now expect to *be* entertained. The program *is* the entertainment. The amusement is in *us*. But others can and must be our entertainers. Now, of course, there is a flourishing "entertainment industry." We generally do not consider book publishing to be part of it.

This is something to reflect on. It is another clue to our special need for libraries. The more omnipresent is the industry that tries to entertain us, the more we need libraries—where pleasure and amusement are found by the free and active spirit.

It is a cliché of our time that what this nation needs is an "informed citizenry." By which we mean a citizenry that is up on the latest information, that has not failed to read this week's newsmagazine, today's newspapers, or to watch the seven o'clock news (perhaps also the news at ten o'clock!)—always for more information, always to be better informed.

I wonder if that is what we need. I suggest, rather, that what we need—what any free country needs—is a *knowledgeable* citizenry. Information, like entertainment, is something someone else provides us. It really is a "service." We expect to be entertained, and also to be informed. *But we cannot be knowledged!* We must all acquire knowledge for ourselves. Knowledge comes from the free mind foraging in the rich pastures of the whole everywhere-past. It comes from finding order and meaning in the whole human experience. The autonomous reader, amusing and knowledging himself, is the be-all and end-all of our libraries.

An Open National Library

Foreword to *Treasures of the Library of Congress*
by Charles A. Goodrum
(New York: Harry N. Abrams, Inc., 1980)

It was difficult for Daniel Boorstin to contain his pride about the Library and its collections; he was its most effective "booster." As part of his determination to share the Library with the rest of the world, he encouraged the writing and publication of a book about the Library, one that would share knowledge of the nature of its collections with the rest of the world. Treasures of the Library of Congress was written by Charles A. Goodrum, and the Librarian of Congress wrote a foreword to it. In this lucid statement, Boorstin concentrated on "what is remarkably American about this kind of national treasury."

WHEN you walk casually into the Library of Congress and ask to see one of these treasures you may not realize that you are doing something which you could not do in other national libraries of the world. Here you need no credentials. I often receive letters from scholars and librarians abroad vouching for the character and scholarly qualities of some particular person, who, they request, should be allowed to use the Library of Congress. The other day as I walked through the Main Reading Room I met a young scholar from England who was deep in our books—even before his "letter of recommendation" had reached me!

This is your Library. The citizens of other countries cannot feel quite the same way about their national libraries. Even in the free world, admission to use the collections of the national library is commonly limited to advanced scholars properly recommended. In the unfree world, the use of the national library is restricted even further—to people who are politically "reliable." There, numerous books are shown only to people who would not be apt to harbor "dangerous thoughts."

The welcome you receive today in your Library of Congress is rooted in American history. Other great national libraries grew out of private collections of kings, nobles, and aristocrats. For example, the magnificent Bibliothèque Nationale in Paris originated in the collections made by early French kings, from the time of Charlemagne. The libraries of Charles V and the House of Orleans were enlarged by Francis I, transferred to Paris by Charles IX, and then expanded by Louis XIV. Of course this explains their treasure trove of early manuscripts and old books, but it also explains an enduring tradition of collecting for the wealthy, the powerful, and the learned. The British Museum (now the British Library) in London has a similar history. It was founded in the personal collections of Sir Hans Sloane (physician to George II) and a few other learned aristocrats, and especially in the personal libraries of George II and George III. You still need a letter of introduction to be admitted to their elegant Reading Room.

The Library of Congress enjoys a more democratic lineage. As the name reminds us, our national collections grew out of an effort, at our nation's founding, to gather knowledge for the people's representatives. To call this the Library of *Congress*, then, is more than a mere matter of nomenclature. And, although it is not widely noted, our name also reveals that the role and the reach of our national library is wider and more open than libraries elsewhere which purport to serve their nations. Our national library remains a possession of the people, made by the people and for the people, and open to the people.

If this Library had its roots in any one personal collection, it was the library of Thomas Jefferson, citizen of the whole world of science, prophet of an expansive representative democracy, and advocate of universal education. "There is, in fact," Jefferson explained, "no subject to which a member of Congress may not have occasion to refer." "Enlighten the people generally," he urged, "and tyranny and oppressions of body and mind will vanish like evil spirits at the dawn of day." An open national library, taking all knowledge for its province and a whole nation as its audience, is a symbol and an instrument of a free people and their own government. When you consult any book in your national collections, you speak volumes about our nation and ourselves.

Most other great national libraries are primarily collections in the official language or languages of their nation. But here in the Library of Congress, nearly three-quarters of the books and a large proportion of other materials are in languages other than English. This is no accident—nor is it an extravagance. On the contrary, this too expresses the special character of our nation.

Recently at an international meeting of national libraries, I was taxed by a librarian from France with the American "megalomania." Why should the Library of the United States, alone among the world's libraries, set about collecting in *all* languages? Other nations have substantially satisfied themselves with materials in their own national languages or about their own country. Why should not the USA also be reasonable, and confine its major collections to works in the "American" language or about the United States? The answer, of course, again lies in our past, and in the unique character of American civilization. If the history of the United States had been like that of France, then we too might have been satisfied with a national stock of books in our own "national" language.

Our history has been radically different. Even English, our official language, has been an import. Our country has been peopled (and, fortunately, continues to be peopled) with immigrants from all over the world. For most of the comers to the United States, English (or "American") has been a second language. Our history bears vivid witness to the fact that people can learn all sorts of new ways of life—including a new spoken language. How, then, could we pretend to make a truly national library for our United States unless we collected in the languages that millions spoke when they arrived—and still arrive—on these shores? And unless we gathered materials on all the civilizations of the world from which Americans have come, and out of which our American civilization has been made? In the United States, of all nations of earth, our *national* library (like our people) must be *international*. This is our proud national paradox, dramatized here in our Library of Congress.

Most other national libraries consist of printed matter and manuscripts. But the Library of Congress's eighteen million volumes are only one-quarter of our items. As the reader of this book will discover, some of our most valued and most remarkable treasures are not manuscripts or books at all. The wonderful miscellany that comprises three-quarters of our inventory includes maps, musical recordings, lithographs, posters, photographs, motion-picture films, computer tapes, microforms, and numerous other formats. The Copyright Law of 1976 made this Library our national archive of radio and television broadcasts.

Yet, when the first Library of Congress building was completed, the Library was expected to collect only books, maps, prints, and manuscripts. As our technologies have grown, so has our Library. Television and the computer are not the last, but only the latest American technology that will enrich our nation's library. If we are to provide a continuous, up-to-date record of our astonishing American civilization, we cannot stay stuck in the old pigeonholes. Of course, we must be grateful for the Book, which the Library's Center for the Book celebrates. We must remain the world's greatest treasury of books. But this technological nation's library must be alert to all the new expressions of civilization. We must seek the whole experience—whatever has filled the consciousness of Americans past and present. And we cannot understand the meaning of the new unless we know what life was like before. Other nations, whose experience has not yet been so transformed by technology, may be satisfied with a library of manuscripts and books. But not the USA!

Our kind of nation thrives not only on Gross National

Product but on Gross National Happiness. We are the only nation, so far as I know, that has included among its declared purposes, "the pursuit of happiness." A library which gathered only the materials of instruction and of high culture would not be true to our heritage. Our national birth certificate, the Declaration of Independence, not only declares that the pursuit of happiness is one of man's "inalienable rights," it goes much further and says that whenever any government ceases to secure those rights, it is the right of the people to alter or abolish it. In the United States the pursuit of happiness is everybody's business, and any American institution which forgets that, is failing in its mission.

The Library of Congress recently mounted an exhibit of a half-century of animated cartoons. On that occasion we rendered to Mickey Mouse and his fellow creatures of the animated world honors which other nations reserve for their priests, potentates, and soccer players. Satisfying and stimulating the American desire to pursue happiness has created a few heroes, a host of celebrities, and countless prosperous businesses. These are more reasons why we must provide and report on all formats—old and new—photographs, motion-picture films, art prints, musical recordings, radio, and television, among others. Collecting, preserving, cataloging and diffusing information about all these materials, as Charles A. Goodrum shows so well, is serious business. Still, we must avoid being solemn, for while we increase knowledge, it is also our duty to increase happiness.

On a scale unequaled by any other library, the Library of Congress opens avenues to knowledge and amusement for those who need special formats. Our service for the blind and physically handicapped, by publications in braille and talking books, and by research into new technologies, opens our treasures to millions more.

The growth, variety, and modernity of the Library is revealed in our three magnificent buildings on Capitol Hill. The first Library of Congress building is itself a unique treasure. The sculpture, painting, and eloquent inscriptions you see here still provide a delightful architectural encyclopedia of the meaning of civilization in 1897. The second Library of Congress building, completed in 1939, larger in capacity than the first, was designed to hold more millions of books and manuscripts. The new Madison Memorial Building, even larger than both the earlier buildings together, now provides services and houses materials never imagined when the first building was opened. In addition to the Congressional Research Service, it offers unexcelled facilities for the storage, preservation, and study of manuscripts, motion-picture films, and musical recordings. Here are three grand monuments to the American people's awe and reverence for their national treasures. The expanding collections, the multiplying media—and the new Madison Building—have given us the opportunity to arrange our collections into a grand Multi-Media Encyclopedia. Technologies, old and new, will help us make the nation's riches more visible, more accessible, and more usable.

These treasures of the Library of Congress did not drop from the sky into their present locations. They were all acquired for us from authors, or composers, or artists seeking copyrights or from somebody else at one time or another. Two remarkable women helped make possible the Library's music collections and performances. Mrs. Elizabeth Sprague Coolidge, herself a noted concert pianist, gave us the Coolidge Auditorium, an acoustical gem unexcelled for chamber music. Mrs. Gertrude Clarke Whittall gave us our five splendid Stradivari instruments (and for each a Tourte bow) requesting that the instruments be played regularly for public enjoyment. Some of our rarest books were the gift of the inspired and generous bibliophile Lessing J. Rosenwald, who not only loved books but loved all who loved books.

The keepers of the treasury, those who have attracted, collected, cataloged, cared for, and served up the nation's treasures, must not be forgotten. Here is the harvest of devoted thousands of men and women, past and present, who have worked in the Library of Congress. With our other benefactors, they have built this treasury and they keep it alive and growing.

A Nation of Readers

Remarks at an Exhibition Opening at the Library of Congress, April 21, 1982

"Reading is not simply a skill or a consumer activity. It is an experience and it has been part of our whole national experience," Boorstin said in his remarks at the opening of "A Nation of Readers," an exhibition illustrating the significance of reading in American life. At the conclusion of his talk he insisted that *"we must raise a citizenry who are qualified to choose their experiences for themselves, from the books past and present, and so secure the independence that only the reader can enjoy."* The phrase "A Nation of Readers" has become one of the Center for the Book's most popular reading promotion themes.

*T*HE pundits in every age have been quick with premature obituaries. When the printed book spread across Europe, learned men forecast the vulgarization of knowledge and the decline of culture. The Renaissance followed. When people from all over came to the United States, our English friends forecast the corruption of their language. But here immigrants from everywhere learned a common tongue, enriched it into an American language of unexcelled vitality, and produced an American renaissance of English literature. When radio appeared, David Sarnoff had difficulty persuading his knowledgeable business colleagues that anybody would want to send messages that were not directed to a specific addressee. We, the anonymous, involuntary recipients of radio and television messages, know how wrong they were.

Every new movement, every new technology, spawns predictions of cataclysm or disaster. In the United States, the most changeful, technologically innovative nation in history, we have had our share of Cassandras. The telephone, some confidently predicted, would soon abolish the mails. The human body could not stand the breathtaking spread of the railroads. Automobiles, Henry Ford was warned, would cause chaos on the roads by frightening all the horses. Still, at heart, American love change and welcome the newer even if it is not always the better. And our enthusiasm for change has actually led us to exaggerate our power to displace the old by the new. The obvious example in our time is the common prediction that television and the computer will displace the book, that a nation of watchers will cease to be a Nation of Readers.

In these few minutes tonight I would like to remind us of some peculiarities of American history which shape what we mean when we Americans speak of a Nation of Readers. We are describing opportunities, risks, and experiences—different from those anywhere else or at any other time. For reading is not simply a skill or a consumer activity. It is an experience and it has been part of our whole national experience. This New World nation has been a crossroads where not only people but technologies meet.

The American public school, in its New England beginnings, taught children to read (and to believe) their *New England Primers*, which eventually sold 5 million copies. In the mid-nineteenth century, texts prepared by William Holmes Mc-Guffey (1800–1873)—himself an American phenomenon with little formal education who at thirteen years of age was teaching on the frontier—dominated American elementary schools for decades, taught reading along with morality and patriotism, and sold 125 million copies. American public schools, especially in the cities, were a crossroads of peoples, where pupils learned to read the American language, which they taught to their immigrant parents. The United States became a nation as it became a Nation of Readers.

For the diffusion of reading matter across our nation no institution (not even our schools) was more powerful than the mails. But only gradually were they permitted to carry

books. Postmaster Return J. Meigs in 1814 forbade the mailing
of books because, he explained, "the mails were . . . overcrowded with novels and the lighter kind of books for
amusement." But he was beset by more pressing problems,
such as the theft of newspapers from the mails and the
mailing of wet newspapers which were a heavy burden to
stagecoach contractors. For decades publishers had to devise
ingenious evasions, such as publishing novels in newspaper
format so they could secure the cheap postage rates allowed
only for newspapers. Meanwhile, the circulation of abolitionist
printed matter had created problems in the South, dramatized
when former Senator Robert Hayne led a mob in Charleston,
South Carolina, invaded the post office, and burned the
publications that offended them.

It was 1851 before books were admitted to the mails and
given special postage rates. In the very next year, 1852, when
Uncle Tom's Cabin was published and then carried by the
mails all across the North, the postal service helped bring on
the Civil War. By 1885 new laws for mailing printed matter
simplified the collection of postage on newspapers and created
a new third class for books. This so effectively promoted the
publication and circulation of reading matter that in 1891
Postmaster General John Wanamaker calculated the annual
weight of dime-novel paperbacks and similar serials at more
than fifty thousand tons. One publisher alone was sending
sixteen hundred tons of paperbacks through the mail annually.
Then in the 1890s Rural Free Delivery widened the flood of
printed matter. In the year 1911, more than a billion newspapers and magazines were delivered to farm homes over
rural mail routes. RFD was christened, with only slight
exaggeration, "the great university in which 36 million of our
people received their daily lessons from the newspapers and
magazines of the country."

The history of how we, a people spread across a continent,
have become a Nation of Readers is of course a history of the
U.S. Mails. It is also a history of transportation in our United
States where technologies of transportation have been re-

markably precocious. This new nation by mid-nineteenth century had more railroad mileage than all of Europe. Much of it went westward, and many lines ran, as puzzled European observers remarked, "from nowhere in particular to nowhere at all." The automobile grew with similar suddenness, and millions of Model Ts were being produced before the roads were there. The rise of the quick lunch (now rechristened fast food) was only one symptom of an America preoccupied with speed—a nation in a hurry, eager for change, anxious for the latest word about everything. The history of the mails and the growth of reading in the United States, then, is largely a drama of our bias for speedy, useful information. And incidentally it is a story of the unending struggle of book publishers to secure the same preferential treatment for books (the wisdom of the ages) which was accorded to newspapers and magazines (the facts and rumors of yesterday and today).

Of course other agencies have promoted and spread reading matter across our nation, and these too have grown with dizzying speed. In 1875 there were only 188 public libraries in eleven states, but in the next quarter-century the public library became one of the most characteristic American educational institutions. By 1900 they numbered five thousand; today there are some nine thousand public library *systems* with countless branches and outposts. In this century a newly characteristic American institution for the diffusion of books has been the book club. The Book-of-the-Month Club, founded in 1926, and the Literary Guild, founded about the same time, were pioneers. By 1965 the total book-club sales were second only to the combined sales of all technical and professional books and had far out-paced adult trade sales, juvenile book sales, and religious book sales. The 9 book clubs in 1928 multiplied until today there are 113 adult book clubs and 21 juvenile book clubs large enough to be listed in *Literary Market Place*.

Meanwhile, of course, retail book outlets—in wholesome competitive rivalry with the book clubs—have multiplied and taken new forms. The neighborhood bookstore which we all love and need, as any reader of *Publishers Weekly* knows, has had problems of survival. But there have been growing outlets in department stores, supermarkets, drugstores, and airports—in addition to the large chains of Dalton, Waldenbooks, and others. The familiar statistics of book publishing show an increase in new titles from some eleven thousand in 1950 to about forty thousand this year.

Tonight, as we celebrate what are or might be the benefits and delights of a Nation of Readers, I would like to suggest some of our peculiar temptations. How can a Nation of Readers find refuge from the narrowing biases of our time?

First, the bias of presentism. Modern communications— from the telegraph and the telephone to television—have increased the emphasis on our daily experience, on the recent and the present—on news-scoops and newsbreaks, on the latest words and images. Most of what we learn from day to day is certified by its immediacy. We learn more and more before it can be put into print, and even before anyone has reflected on whether it is worth knowing. By the time it is put into print it would be obsolete or proven false. But this is an old story in our country. The whole American experience from colonial times—when the current and the useful, almanacs, the latest laws and newspapers and pamphlets and how-to-do-it manuals dominated the presses—through the many decades of the postal rates which have almost always preferred newspapers and magazines to books—American institutions have been biased toward the recent and the up-to-date, toward information rather than knowledge.

This bias of American printed matter was reinforced by the gargantuan enterprise and spectacular growth of American daily newspapers in the nineteenth century. And it has been reinforced a hundredfold by the rising electronic media. A nation of watchers has its eyes focused on yesterday and today. Even our entertainment is no longer tragedy or comedy but *situations*—which get tears or laughter from the quagmires of this very moment. But book-readers have a window to the whole past. Every book has its roots at least six months ago. The full stock of all past books is available to all of us

without special programming or the use of artificially ener-
gized, obsolescing machinery. Every book-reader can find
momentary refuge from the present.

Second, the bias of publicity. Just as we are more than ever
flooded by images and sounds of the present, so we are
dominated by publicly spoken words. Public utterances are
more numerous, more frequent, and more public than ever
before. The sunshine laws make the private conferences of
our highest officials a new kind of public word. When the
President and the Secretary of State have a private conversation
it is presented verbatim in the day's newspapers. The public
word and the public speaker reach us vividly and continually,
aided by large expenditures of capital, by large organizations,
on channels regulated from within and without. More than
ever each of us needs a private island where each of us does
his own programming, and where only one person, each of
us, is sovereign.

Third, the bias of statistics. Not the least of the special
charms for a reader today is refuge from the quantifiable. Of
course we have our best-sellers, but who can say what books
really are the best read? While the TV audience is increasingly
Nielsen-rated, the reader and his ways remain delightfully
secret and mysterious. We have heard the boast that on one
evening of John Gielgud's *Hamlet* on TV more people saw
Shakespeare's play than all the audiences together since 1604.
But who can count Hamlet's readers? GNP and statistics of
consumption can tell us about automobiles and appliances
and cigarettes, but very little about reading. A book read is
not consumed. And surely some of the best read books do
not enter into this year's or last year's publishing figures. The
reader continues to "consume" models from the horse-and-
buggy days or before, from the Model-T era, or from last
year, sometimes without noticing which. For each of us our
reading remains a private, uniquely qualitative nook of our
life. As readers, then, we are refugees from the flood of
contemporaneous mathematicized homogeneity. There we
are at home with ourselves.

To have the benefits of a Nation of Readers, we must have

citizens who can read. Our first assignment is not to allow the published electronic image or the public word to deter us in the primary effort of our education. We must raise a citizenry who are qualified to choose their experience for themselves, from the books past and present, and so secure the independence that only the reader can enjoy.

When we think of the role of words in our nation's political life, prominent in our minds are famous utterances—Burke's Speech on Conciliation, Patrick Henry's "Give me liberty or give me death," Webster's reply to Hayne, Lincoln's Gettysburg Address, Bryan's "Cross of Gold" speech, or Franklin Delano Roosevelt's "We have nothing to fear but fear itself." Representative government, universal suffrage, and a host of technological forces, especially in the United States, have focused our political interest on the public speaker. The building across the street from this Library of Congress has reverberated with many of the nation's great public utterances.

It is symbolically appropriate, and even necessary, here on Capitol Hill that we find two grand buildings, one a temple of the spoken word, another a temple of the read word. One is a symbol of the publicity essential to a free government. The other, a symbol of the privacy essential to a free people.

Books in Our Future

Excerpts from *Books in Our Future: A Report from the Librarian of Congress to the Congress*, Joint Committee on the Library, 1984

> On November 18, 1983, Congress approved Senate Concurrent Resolution 59, which authorized a study of the changing role of the book in the future, to be carried out by the Librarian of Congress under the auspices of the Center for the Book. The Librarian's report, published late in 1984, drew on discussions with a twenty-person Advisory Committee on the Book in the Future, but the conclusions were his. Excerpts are presented below.

*W*E AMERICANS have a habit of writing premature obituaries. Our love of novelty and our speedy pace of change tempt us to imagine that the new technology buries the old. A century ago some predicted that the telegraph and the telephone would spell the end of the postal system. Television of course brought prophecies of the demise of radio. In this century more than once we have heard enthusiasts for a new technology predict the demise of the book. When the automobile first became popular some actually said that few Americans would stay home reading when they could be riding the countryside in their flivvers. The rise of photography, phonography, and the movies led others to foresee the disappearance of the book from the classroom. It would be displaced, they said, by the latest "audiovisual aids." But today textbooks still dominate the classroom.

The Culture of the Book

Meanwhile, books in their traditional form encompass us in a thousand ways. Each of our major religions is a religion of the book, with sacred texts that are the source and the vehicle of theology, morality, and hopes for the future. Our education has been built around books. The structure of our political life rests on our books of law, history, geography, and biography. Books are the main source of our knowledge, our reservoir of faith, memory, wisdom, morality, poetry, philosophy, history, and science.

The book-stored wisdom of the Bible, Locke, Burke, Blackstone, and the great authors of the European liberal tradition was the foundation for the grand experiment of our Founding Fathers. They put the free access to printed matter, along with freedom of religion, among the first items of the first article in the Bill of Rights of our Constitution. "I cannot live without books," declared Thomas Jefferson after his books were shipped from Monticello to become the foundation of the renewed Library of Congress in 1815. And at once he began building a new personal library. Without books we might be tempted to believe that our civilization was born yesterday—or when the latest newsmagazine went to press. The very omnipresence of books leads us to underestimate their power and influence. One measure of their meaning to mankind is the desperate hunger of people in unfree societies to read everything that is not government-authorized pap.

It is no accident that people everywhere have considered books sacred and have made them the source and the vehicle of their religious faith. For the power of the book has been uncanny, mysterious, inestimable, overpowering, and infinite—just as the activity of reading has a unique individuality, intimacy, and privacy.

Our civilization is a product of the Culture of the Book. Of course, the book itself—the printed, bound volume—is a triumph of technology. But when we speculate on the future of the traditional book we are not thinking about a single product of technology. Never since the discovery of fire and the invention of the wheel has any other innovation had so pervasive and so enduring an influence on ways of thinking, feeling, worshipping, teaching, governing, and discovering.

The revolution since Gutenberg is without precedent. Its consequences are yet to be seen in much of the world. This effect, in Thomas Carlyle's familiar words, was "disbanding hired armies, and cashiering most kings and senates, and creating a whole new democratic world."

We all have an enormous vested interest in the book. The Library of Congress possesses some 18 million volumes, accumulated over two centuries at a cost of hundreds of millions of dollars. In the United States today there are more than 100,000 libraries—federal, state, and city, public, special, school, and institutional—which house at least 200 million volumes, constantly increasing. The Library of Congress alone receives 1,000 new volumes from all over the world every day.

We see books everywhere, of every conceivable variety, in homes and schools, in offices and workshops. Not only Bibles, prayer books, dictionaries, encyclopedias, and textbooks, but also novels, books of mystery, romance, travel, nature, and adventure, and children's books, along with how-to-do-it books on sewing, car repair, home maintenance, computers, gardening, athletics, and health, not to mention telephone books, mail-order catalogs, and company directories. Books are everyday fixtures of our lives, guides and measures of our civilization. To try to extract the book from our lives would be fatal, but luckily this is impossible.

Our long investment in books is only one reason to expect the book to remain a fertile resource in the America of the next decades. The proverbial convenience, accessibility, and individuality of the book are unrivaled now or by any new technology in sight. The book is independent of outside power sources, and offers unique opportunities for freedom of choice. "One reads at one's own speed," Vincent Canby reminds us, "in short snatches on the subway or in long, voluptuous withdrawals from the world. One proceeds through a big, complex novel, say *War and Peace*, or *Crime and Punishment*, like an exceptionally well-heeled tourist in a foreign landscape, going slowly or fast depending on the roads, on one's own mood and on the attractions along the way. If one loses something, one can always go back to pick it up." For all these reasons, books are messengers of freedom. They can be hidden under a mattress or smuggled into slave nations.

We Americans have never been inclined to underestimate new technologies, nor have we held on sentimentally to the ways of our grandparents. Our faith in obsolescence comes from the amazingly speedy changes in our ways of life. Naturally, then, we enjoy science-fiction fantasies of a world of microchips, where our library-store of books has become obsolete and our personal bookshelves unnecessary. For we eagerly discard the old if there seems a newer, more interesting—even if more complicated—way of doing the same task. Rube Goldberg gave us an eloquent slogan for our national way of life: "Do It the Hard Way!"

The Twin Menaces: Illiteracy and Aliteracy

New technologies are new allies in our national effort to inform and educate Americans. We must enlist the new technologies with cautious enthusiasm. The threat to a knowledgeable citizenry is not from new technology. But there is a threat from our hasty readiness to exaggerate or misconceive the promise of new technologies, which carries the assumption that the Culture of the Book is a thing of the past. Today we are failing to do all we should do to qualify young Americans to read and so draw on the main storehouse of our civilization. We are failing to provide enough access to books. And we can do much more to increase the motivation to read.

We must face and defeat the twin menaces of illiteracy and aliteracy—the inability to read and lack of the will to read—if our citizens are to remain free and qualified to govern themselves. We must aim to abolish illiteracy in the United States by 1989.

Combining Technologies: The Adaptable Book

The culture of the book will continue to be enriched by new technologies. The traditional book, of course, lacks the novelty, commercial hype, and futuristic romance that surround more recent technologies of communication. While exploding newer technologies have excited popular attention and the interest of the newspaper and magazine press, interest in reading, enthusiasm for books, and the prosperity of the book-publishing industry have remained relatively stable. Today about half of all adult Americans read books and their number is not declining. Of these, more than a third are heavy readers of books, and that proportion is increasing. The staying power of the traditional book is astonishing.

Until the twentieth century the advances of media technology aimed mainly at wider, speedier, and more economical diffusion of printed words and images. The technology of recent decades has added new and complementary dimensions to our experience. Photography has enlivened books by authentic pictures and portraits. The phonograph has preserved and diffused the voices of statesmen, singers, and poets and the virtuoso performances of musicians. Motion pictures have kept alive images of the past and have translated books into newly vivid moving, talking images. Radio has widened the audience beyond time and space and added new opportunities for entertainment, suspense, information, news, and instruction. Television, which some said would mark the demise of opera, has instead given opera a new life and vast new audiences. And, of course, television has made every home a theater, a showcase, a museum, a newsroom, and a classroom. Optical disk technology promises to help us combine earlier technologies to open new vistas to scholars and citizens.

New Technologies Bring More Readers

Each of these technologies has created new inducements to read books. The plays of Shakespeare, Chekhov, Ibsen, Shaw, Arthur Miller, and Tennessee Williams, the novels of Dickens, Dumas, Hugo, Flaubert, Tolstoy, Hardy, Orwell, and Mann enjoy revival in libraries and bookstores with their reappearance in movies or on the television screen. Popular screenplays or series written for television themselves become a new raw material for mass-market paperbacks. Publishers' records show that the television series based on Alex Haley's *Roots* and Herman Wouk's *Winds of War* attracted thousands of new buyers and readers of these books. Evelyn Waugh's *Brideshead Revisited*, first published in 1945, had a renaissance in American bookstores in 1983 when it became a television series. "Reading Rainbow," a television series funded by the Corporation for Public Broadcasting and the Kellogg Company to encourage reading among children ages five to nine, has sold hundreds of thousands of copies of books on which the programs were based. Books on cassettes can entice new readers. The computer itself has provided a popular subject matter for books. R. R. Bowker's new *Retailers' Microcomputer Market Place* will list over six thousand books and five hundred periodicals about computers.

New Technologies Serve Scholarship and Humanistic Culture

New technology plays new scholarly roles. For decades, microfilming projects have preserved texts of books, journals, and newspapers and made research collections widely available. Scientists at the Crocker Nuclear Laboratory at the University of California at Davis are using a cyclotron to analyze the ink on a fifteenth-century Bible. Scholars at the Clark Library of the University of California at Los Angeles are developing microcomputer programs for textual criticism and editing. The latest and by far the best concordance to Shakespeare has been made by computer. The capture of the sixty million words of the monumental *Oxford English Dictionary* by computer will make the production of all future editions faster, more economical, and more up-to-date. Our leading American dictionaries and encyclopedias now use computer technology to ease revision, to make new words, novel meanings, and new articles readily available to the public.

Each new technology changes the environment for the

Culture of the Book. Multiplying media have deprived the printed word of its traditional monopoly on access to knowledge, information, and the masterpieces of civilization. For at least a century, speedily innovating technology has multiplied enticing distractions and increased competition for the time and energy and money once devoted to buying and reading books. The telephone, phonograph, radio, and television and their portable, wearable forms, have made the silence that facilitates reading harder than ever to find. But they have also made the boundless choices and personalized experience of the book more welcome and more necessary.

The Mirage of "Computer Literacy"

Meanwhile, the American enthusiasm for the newest is betrayed in our everyday vocabulary. People never spoke of movie-literacy, radio-literacy, or television-literacy. *Literacy*, "the ability to read and write," was assumed to be the prime requisite for a free people. It carried with it the capacity and the opportunity to select one's own sources of knowledge and to enjoy a private, individualized experience of pleasure and self-instruction. Now we hear pleas for "computer-literacy"! Here is a telltale clue to the continuing kudos of the book as the main avenue to knowledge. This expression also shows how we fuzzy over our culture with fashionable ambiguities. Our enthusiasm for "computer-literacy"—the ability to manipulate the latest model of this latest device—seems about to overshadow our concern for book-literacy. But mastering a machine is no substitute for the ability to read, and computer competence itself depends on the ability to read. Schools and summer camps and correspondence courses aim to make "computer-literates" out of people who remain ill at ease in the world of books.

To keep our thinking straight and our culture alive and our people free we must keep our definition of literacy sharp and clear. To use computers effectively requires a familiarity with books and a friendliness to books. We have yet to find a feasible alternative to the ability to learn from the printed word and enjoy the boundless treasures. The book is always "user friendly." We must aim to make all Americans book friendly.

The Alliance of Technologies

The same human ingenuity that produced the book has produced later technologies, and they are all allies. Our task is to recognize and promote their alliance. We must see the role which the computer is already playing and that which it is likely to play. Then we will not underestimate or abandon book-literacy. The enemy of the book is not technology but the illusion that we could or would abolish the Culture of the Book.

There is no end to our hopes for devices to spread the benefits and pleasures (and frustrations) of technology to our whole nation, including our children in school. While people in older worlds, confronted with a new technology, have been inclined to ask "Why?" we Americans have usually asked "Why not?" Our false prophets have been those who declared that something was impossible. The telegraph, telephone, phonograph, radio, television, nuclear energy—and now the computer—all violated the confident "impossibilities" of the experts. Therefore as we speculate about the Book in the Future we must not dare to prophesy that *anything* will be impossible here. The miracles of the computer will be supplemented by others more astonishing. Yet we must not allow our innovating hopes and enthusiasms to dazzle us. We must do our fallible best to suggest the extent and the limits of the roles of the new computer technology.

Unexplored Opportunities

But we need not await future technologies to find new opportunities for enriching the Culture of the Book. During World War II a standard format was used for printing the

Armed Services Editions—little oblong paperback reprints, of which nearly 123 million copies were distributed free. These 1,322 titles were produced in wartime at a cost of about six cents each. The project required the cooperation not only of the Armed Services but of the War Production Board, seventy publishing firms, a dozen printing houses and composition firms, paper suppliers, and scores of authors. Millions of readers in uniform found enlightenment and good cheer from a menu that included Katherine Anne Porter, Robert Benchley, Lytton Strachey, Max Brand, E. B. White, Leo Rosten, Herman Wouk, Budd Schulberg, and Graham Greene and in moods that range from *The Education of Henry Adams* to *McSorley's Wonderful Saloon*. The Armed Services Editions proved to be one of the greatest cultural bonanzas in American history. They stirred the reading appetites of millions who would never lose their taste for books. They required a minimum of technological innovation and a maximum of imagination and organizing talent. It is not surprising that a vast new market for paperback books appeared after the war.

If so grand an enterprise could be accomplished under the constraints of a wartime economy, surely we today are capable of enterprises of comparable grandeur. Many opportunities come from our fantastically multiplying media. Television, which so thoroughly reaches into every American home, offers unprecedented means to whet appetites for reading among Americans of all ages. A few projects, like "Reading Rainbow" and the "Read More About It" project of the Library of Congress and CBS, with its slogan "linking the pleasure, power, and excitement of books and television," have begun to use television to invigorate the Culture of the Book. Still, such projects are too few. We need many more of them to keep our citizens in touch with our whole human heritage and so fulfill anew the hopes for enlightenment on which our nation was founded.

When printing from movable type was first invented in Europe it was praised as the *ars artium omnium conservatrix* ("the art preservative of all the arts"). In our age, we can reap the harvest of a half-millennium of the printed word. We must not forget that for us reading books is "the activity which enriches all others." There is no business, work, sport, skill, entertainment, art, or science that cannot be improved by reading and whose rewards cannot be increased by books. The reading of books, as we have seen, is not a passive, marginal social fact but a major national activity. We must use all our technologies to make the most of our inheritance, to move toward an American Renaissance of the Culture of the Book.

Will America Live without Books?

Statement at the Library of Congress on the occasion
of the publication of *Books in Our Future: A Report
from the Librarian of Congress to the Congress,*
December 6, 1984

*"As inheritors of the wisdom of Adams and Jefferson and Madison,
the eponyms of our Library of Congress Buildings, [the Library of
Congress] must be both Pro-Technology and Pro-Book,"* Librarian
Boorstin declared in his remarks. He also used the occasion to
announce two important ways in which Congress had *"concretely
and dramatically expressed confidence in the Library of Congress
and in the survival of our wonderfully mixed technologies."* These
were: large appropriations for a book preservation facility and
financial support for the restoration and renovation of the Jefferson
Building.

$\mathcal{T}$ONIGHT we focus on two mysteries, not often celebrated
together. We usually associate books with the past, its products
and pleasures, dramas and treasures. But tonight we think
about books in our future.

The book—the mysteriously versatile book—in its traditional form is both the most concrete and the most abstract
of objects. A small book can be put under the leg of a wobbly
table, or can provide texts for prayers to our Creator. A large
book can be a doorstop or, on a chair in our dining room,
can lift our children and grandchildren to a comfortable
height, and yet it can be an encyclopedic guide to the worlds
of art, philosophy, and literature. A book can be as ephemeral
as the paperbacks which dissolve from airport counters every
three weeks, or as enduring as the dialogues of Plato and the

wisdom of the Bible. It can spread the petrified lies of dictators, or carry the free-flowing ideas of a democratic republic. It can bind enslaved people in phlegmatic acquiescence, or it can stir them to revolt. Historically speaking, a book is a kind of everything and anything.

Nor is the future—the mysteriously problematic future—a realm of clear boundaries or simple dimensions. The future can be as certain as a statistic or an extrapolation—as definite as the population growth projected by the Bureau of the Census or the pollsters' prediction of election returns with only minute margins of error. Or it can be as uncertain as next month's interest rates. It is as predictable as progress and as unpredictable as the machines of progress.

Yet we cannot evade the doubly elusive question. In the future, will America live without books? We must face this question not only because the Congress has posed it to us, but for other reasons too. We Americans, in this most technologically advanced nation of the world, in recent years have suffered a peculiarly acute attack of an epidemic, recurrent American disease. I call it technological utopianism. This is not the simple, familiar faith in technology which all human beings have shared since the invention of the wheel, of language, and the alphabet. Ours is rather a pathological myopia, an obsession with the *latest* technology, whatever it has happened to be.

As our report to the Congress suggests, we live in a Culture of the Book, where our religions, our education, our laws, our science, our access to the long human past and to the delights of the human imagination all come by way of alphabetic print on paper, the book in its traditional form. Here in the Library of Congress alone we possess some eighteen million such objects, which cannot economically be transposed to any other form yet in sight.

The traditional book still has an unrivaled privacy, convenience, portability, and accessibility. Yet the book itself is, of course, a triumph of technology. And its uses, too, are transformed by newer technologies. Our report will suggest some areas where the role of the book will be transformed, or even displaced. As Americans and as natural optimists, we must see how the new technologies, including of course the computer, will improve and widen our access to knowledge and information. The Library of Congress has pioneered in these areas. Yet we Americans will not cease to live in a Culture of the Book. As inheritors of the wisdom of Adams and Jefferson and Madison, the eponyms of our Library of Congress buildings, we must be both Pro-Technology and Pro-Book.

We must also be Pro-Future! Americans have never been willing refugees from the problems and opportunities of the present. It would be most un-American for us to yearn for the days before the computer—any more than we could yearn for the days before the alphabet, before movable type, before photography of phonography, or movies or radio or television. Here in America we see that man—often misdescribed as the problem-solving animal—is the problem-inventing animal. Here where every new problem opens the way for ever more risky inventions, we enjoy living on the brink of the future. While the Old World romanticizes the past, our inverted American nostalgia romanticizes the future.

Yet the future creeps in more slowly than we like to imagine. Here in this Great Hall we can see how the architecture, the art, the furniture, and the habits, faiths, and traditions of our past outlast the full-page advertisements and the most vivid commercials. The hallmark of technological progress is obsolescence. The hallmark of books is survival.

Tonight, as we present to the Congress the report they have requested of us on the book in the future, we have with us members of the advisory committee for our report and many others who have contributed. The request itself, which we owe in great part to Senator Mathias, the chairman of the Joint Committee on the Library, who unfortunately cannot be with us tonight, expresses a gratifying confidence in the Library of Congress. It reminds us of our continuing need to assess the relation between the treasures and techniques of our past and the treasures and techniques still hidden in our future. The Congress has more concretely and dramatically expressed confidence in the Library of Congress and in the survival of our wonderfully mixed technologies by appropriating $11.5 million for a building for book-preservation at Fort Detrick, Maryland. There we will treat a half million books each year with a diethyl-zinc compound developed here at the Library, and so extend the life expectancy of these books from decades to centuries. The Congress has made history. Never before have we heard of a building of such proportions for the express purpose of extending the longevity of books into a distant future. And in addition, Congress has appropriated $81.5 million to refurbish this building, to restore its pristine beauty, and to adapt it to the needs of the twentieth and twenty-first centuries, when the nation's library, the world's library, must be a Multi-Media Encyclopedia. Here we will preserve the glory and elegance of our past. Here we will marry technologies and resources old and new. Here we aim to fulfill the hopes of Thomas Jefferson, that in America enlightenment will preserve freedom, and freedom will nourish knowledge.

The Indivisible World: Libraries and the Myth of Cultural Exchange

Remarks at the General Conference of the International Federation of Library Associations (IFLA), Chicago, August 19, 1985

> *"All culture belongs to all people. Books and ideas make a boundless world . . . . To keep that world indivisible is our most urgent difficult task." These words from Boorstin's 1985 IFLA address prefaced a plea for librarians around the world to fight censorship and to work to remove obstacles which impede the flow of books and ideas.*

IN THIS TIME OF political hostilities, military threats, trade barriers, and technological rivalry and secrecy, we must not forget some of the unique features of cultural relations among nations, and the role of libraries, especially of books.

In recent decades we have heard a great deal about so-called Cultural Exchange. Many countries have their cultural foreign service. We have our United States Information Service, the British have their British Council, the French have their Alliance Française, the West Germans have their Goethe Houses, and the Soviet Union has its counterpart. Nowadays embassies have their "cultural attachés"—an expression which entered the English language only in 1937. "Cultural Exchange" has entered the jargon of international relations. And there is not a great deal of difference between the kinds of activities of the countries, however diverse their political or economic philosophies. They send lecturers, musicians, orchestras, dance-groups, and dramatic performers. They all distribute books and maintain libraries. Of course, we librarians have been in the business of international cultural relations for at least two thousand years—ever since Callimachus went to Alexandria to build the famous library's collection, and produced his 120-volume catalog of the holdings in Greek literature.

Nowadays our thinking about these thriving and costly international cultural transactions is governed by some seductive metaphors. These metaphors are borrowed from politics, economics, and military affairs. From politics come the notions of leadership, domination, and compromise, of annexation and national boundaries. From economics come the notions of competition, balance of trade (imports and exports), and reciprocity. From the military come the notions of invasion, conquest, advance and retreat. These all express and foster ways of thinking which, in my opinion, are inappropriate to the world of culture, and especially to the world of books and ideas. They corrupt our thought and distract us from our proper mission as librarians to the world.

All these crudities are expressed in the single notion of Cultural Exchange. As a member of several official commissions on cultural relations between the United States and other countries, I have often met this notion. I have heard intelligent people debate the "reciprocity" of cultural exports and imports. Since so many American movies are exported and shown in India, then, in order to promote cordial relations and a sense of the equality of peoples, must not an equivalent number of movies be imported to the United States from India? May it not be an indignity to the people of India if they send many of their works of sculpture to be exhibited in the United States, unless equivalent works from the Unites States are simultaneously sent for exhibit in India? And what does it show of the Indian people's respect for the United States if what they wish from our great museums are not an equivalent number of works by Americans, but works from our European, Asian, and African collections? Similar debates concerning our relations with other countries go on all the time. In my opinion these are exercises in futility, efforts to compare the incomparable, to measure incommensurables.

This language of cultural equivalents violates the unique character of works of art. It prevents us from recognizing the capacity of all peoples to produce their own kind of uniqueness. In contrast with the commodities of commercial exchange, significant works of art are not quantifiable. Only trivial and evanescent works—pulp music and pulp novels—can be numbered. But how many paintings by Jamini Roy equal how many Jackson Pollocks? How many Hiroshige prints equal how many Whistler etchings?

We know, too, that while we can make useful projections of the gross national product or the output of mines and factories, nothing like that is possible in the realm of the arts. The artist and his works are unpredictable.

Furthermore, we know that, unlike commodities of the marketplace, books and works of art are cumulative and not displacive. If we buy a Honda or a Mercedes we are not apt to buy a Chevrolet or a Cadillac. But if we play Copland or Bartok we do not cease playing Mozart or Beethoven. Reading Virgil enriches our pleasure in Homer. Works of art and literature are iridescent, they take on new meanings from new points of view and in new conditions of our world. Shakespeare, Goethe, and Dostoyevsky tell each generation something new. The uses of an automobile, a camera, or a television set are more fixed and more predictable. A work of art or of literature—a Brueghel or a Van Gogh—a *Paradise Lost* or a *Moby Dick*—is great precisely because it is unique and incommensurable. We cannot know what they may mean to a future generation.

Now, when we turn from the art products of a culture to its ideas, all these elusivenesses are multiplied. The air is never empty of ideas. The atmosphere of our society—of any society—is not a vacuum into which a government or a minister of culture can pour a desired content. It is a copious fertile ether, and, like the Chinese *ch'i*, an inexhaustible source of energy and creation that is found everywhere.

Again, in dramatic contrast to the world of exchangeable commodities, ideas and knowledge are nondepletable. They are indefinitely, even infinitely, expandable. The ideas of idealism or materialism flourish because more people accept them. In fact knowledge increases by diffusion. No patent or copyright—nor any device of government yet contrived—can prevent people from having an idea, from enjoying it, elaborating it, and passing it on to countless others. And there is no precise equivalence among ideas. Ideas are not fungible. One idea cannot take exactly the same place that was held by another.

Like works of art and literature, *ideas* too are cumulative and not displacive. Japanese steel may displace American-made steel from our factories, and a Volvo can displace an Oldsmobile on our roads. But the ideas in Marx's *Das Kapital* built on the ideas in Adam Smith's *Wealth of Nations*, and some think that Marx gave Smith's ideas a new urgency and a new vogue. The ideas have never yet been invented which can drive Plato's ideas out of circulation. Nor are ideas quantifiable. Despite the expectations of professors grading examination papers, can we really say how many ideas there are in Aristotle's *Politics*, or how many ideas have derived from them? Ideas—innumerable, and boundless—are unimaginably fertile.

From these familiar features of art and books and ideas, it must be evident, too, that culture has an inertia, a momentum, and a spontaneity not encompassed in the borrowed jargon of cultural exchange. A book is a uniquely explosive device. But ideas, unlike people, do not exterminate one another. There never was an idea that could not be revived and given new life. Ideas may seem to compete, but no one ever finally wins that competition. So long as people live and think, there will never be an enduring monopoly by any idea. We need no antitrust laws in the world of ideas. The diffusion of any idea—democracy or communism, for example—in the long run will increase man's desire to know other ideas. No government can permanently stultify this appetite.

The boundaries and divisions of nations and states and cities are needed for social services, for water and sewage, for protection of property and the administration of justice. But the cultural world—the world of books and ideas—is indivisible. The barriers needed to direct traffic, to prevent crime, to control drugs, or to promote the domestic economy— these too have no place in the librarians' world. How impoverished would our knowledge and our culture be, if we had access only to books first written in our national language by our fellow nationals!

The world's cultures—and the culture of books—may be defined by languages, by traditions, by historical movements. But they are not confined by national boundaries. Ideas need no passports from their place of origin, nor visas for the countries they enter. All boundaries in the world of culture and ideas are artificial and all are doomed to be dissolved.

We, the librarians of the world, are servants of an indivisible world. Though some of us are national librarians, culture is not national. All culture belongs to all people. Books and ideas make a boundless world. To try to confine the reading or the thinking of any people violates the very nature of culture.

To keep that world indivisible is our most urgent, our most difficult task. Chauvinists—political, economic, or military— would make our libraries narrowly national. And ideologues, claiming the final answer to our finally unanswerable questions, try to sanitize the books that are published, and seek to sterilize the contents of our libraries. These are enemies and saboteurs of our work as the world's librarians.

At the Library of Congress in Washington, D.C., we make an effort to serve an indivisible world of culture and books and ideas. Only about one-quarter of the books on our shelves are in English, the primary language of our country, while three-quarters are in the other languages of our immigrant nation and of the world. More than half our entries are in non-Roman alphabet, including extensive collections in the Slavic languages, Chinese, Japanese, and languages of India and Southeast Asia and Africa. In collecting and preserving other cultural objects—photographs, graphic art, motion pictures, music, and maps—we also try to display the full spectrum of the cultures of mankind. Although the effort is costly and time-consuming, we do our best not to allow ourselves to be confined by the cultures of Europe and the West.

Everywhere our efforts to keep the world of culture and of ideas indivisible face obstacles. Even in the United States we see occasional efforts to censor libraries and confine the reading of our citizens to what some lawmakers or self-appointed arbiters of morals consider wholesome. Luckily, until now, these have been few and have carried little weight. Other countries are not so lucky. In much, perhaps even most of the world today, people are not free to read whatever they like, or whatever the world can send them.

We are pleased to learn that, for example, in the Lenin Library in Moscow more than one-third of the books are in languages other than Russian. But, at the same time, all librarians must be saddened that a new Russian word recently entered our desk dictionaries: "*samizdat* . . . The secret publication and distribution of government-banned literature in the U.S.S.R. . . . The literature produced by this system." How happy we could be someday to see this word disappear from our dictionaries and to learn that the word had become obsolete!

In a world divided by ideology, by trade barriers, by military threats and nuclear fear, we librarians are not powerless. We are the ambassadors of an indivisible world— of culture and books and ideas. Unfortunately, we are not plenipotentiary. But there is no country in the world where librarians, encouraged by a national librarian, cannot make some small progress toward removing the boundaries and lowering the barriers which separate cultures and which are sponsored by citizens or by governments. Every librarian, regardless of his government's policy, has the opportunity, if he has the courage, to open the avenues of books and ideas a little wider.

For librarians there can be no unwholesome ideas or banned books—only unwholesome efforts to limit ideas and stultify the whole world of books. Until every reader in the world has free access to any books from anywhere we librarians have not completed our task. "Librarians of the World, Unite!" We can hope and must try everywhere to make the world of books more open—so that men and women everywhere may breathe freely the uncensored open air of ideas.

Don Quixote in the Age of Television

Remarks at the Library of Congress on October 29, 1985, marking the seventh season of the Library of Congress/CBS Television "Read More About It" Book Project

This occasion, a dinner in the Library's Great Hall, honored the actors and actresses who had presented thirty-second reading messages in the "Read More About It" project, which is coordinated by the Center for the Book. An exhibition about the life and works of Miguel de Cervantes, already on view in the Great Hall, presented the Librarian with a challenging theme for his after-dinner remarks.

SURROUNDING us in the Great Hall is an exhibit of the life and works of Miguel de Cervantes (1547–1616), the great Spanish writer whose *Don Quixote* (1605; 1615) is, except for the Bible, the world's most widely translated book. Here at the Library of Congress we have it in thirty languages. It is no accident that we have scheduled this exhibit to open at the time of the Center for the Book, Library of Congress/CBS Television "Read More About It" celebration. For *Don Quixote* brings a special message to our Age of Television.

Nearly four hundred years ago, Cervantes foresaw the need for the enterprise of CBS in collaboration with the Library of Congress which we celebrate tonight. The Knight of the Sorrowful Countenance in Cervantes's epic was driven to the quixotic adventures which would become bywords around the world by a single kind of overdose. That Ingenious Gentleman Don Quixote de la Mancha, Cervantes explains in his first chapter, "when he was at leisure, which was most of the year around, was in the habit of reading books of chivalry with such pleasure and devotion as to lead him almost wholly to forget the life of a hunter and even the administration of his estate. So great was his curiosity and infatuation in this regard that he even sold many acres of tillable land in order to be able to buy and read the books that he loved, and he would carry home with him as many of them as he could obtain."

The books that obsessed Don Quixote were all of one kind—books of Romance and Chivalry. The effect of this obsession on the respectable gentleman of about fifty years was disastrous. Cervantes explained, "In short, our gentleman became so immersed in reading that he spent whole nights from sundown to sunup and his days from dawn to dusk in poring over his books, until, finally, from so little sleeping and so much reading, his brain was dried up and he went completely out of his mind. He had filled his imagination with everything that he had read, with enchantments, knightly encounters, battles, challenges, wounds, with tales of love and its torments, and all sorts of impossible things, and as a result had come to believe that all these fictitious happenings were true; they were more real to him than anything else in the world." Yet Cervantes was actually not describing a television watcher!

The disastrous consequences for poor Don Quixote were not without benefits for succeeding generations—and for us. Don Quixote's illusions produced an incomparable epic of man's battles with unreality. Cervantes provided the prototype of the modern novel, with a legacy which comes to us through his disciples, from Smollett and Sterne, through Melville, Pushkin, Dostoyevsky, and Herman Wouk, through Richard Strauss and Massenet, Doré and Daumier. Here in the Library of Congress we celebrate that legacy.

It may seem strange that here, of all places, we should celebrate an epic whose moral was the danger of reading too many books. But of course that was not the burden of Don Quixote's madness. His career was not a parable against reading. Nor even against reading books of Romance and

Chivalry. The engrossing nine hundred pages of Don Quixote's adventures are, paradoxically, an advertisement for the fantasies to be enjoyed in those very books. Cervantes's moral was not the danger in books. If that had been his message, he would hardly have spent so much of his life, at such personal sacrifice, with only one good hand at his command, adding to the world's stock of books.

Don Quixote is, rather, a cautionary tale against an overdose of any one kind of book. More precisely, against allowing ourselves to be dominated by any one avenue to the real world. To be human, Cervantes suggests, is to seek all possible avenues to reality—beyond the times and places of our own personal experience. In his time books were the dominating, the most rich and vivid alternative to personal experience. There were no other media. In the days before television, the different genres of books had widely different audiences. In the sixteenth century, if there was any counterpart to television for the wider literate populace, it was probably books of Romance and Chivalry.

Cervantes brings us a warning against any single window on the world. He dramatized the perils even in the revered format of the book. The confusion of *our* sense of reality comes from the newly dominate medium, the newly opened window of our time— which is, of course, television. Cervantes showed that books were not the antidote for the unrealities that books made seem real. In our time, too, the cure for the illusions spawned by television may not be more (or even better) television. We need to keep our other windows open.

Tonight as we celebrate the "Read More About It" program and the statesmanship of CBS in promoting this program, we declare the need for many and varied windows on the world. We dare not risk a nation of TV-Don Quixotes. We Americans must not let our sense of the world be fuzzied over by this newest, most promising, most vivid, most democratic of all media. We face new perils: TV-Myopia, mistaking the image in our living room for the reality out there. TV-Dystopia, mistaking the horrors we see on the screen for the horrors out there. But perhaps worst of all is the same kind of bewilderment which poor Don Quixote suffered and which produced his miseries—the confusion between what the medium (whether books of Romance and Chivalry or television) says is real and what is really real.

We welcome tonight the many artists and performers who have enlivened our days and nights with their performances. By their appearances on "Read More About It," they have served us all in a special way. They have warned the Don Quixotes among us that there are many paths to the world out there. They have brought to life, even into our homes, a countless company of latter-day Knights of the Sorrowful Countenance, of many less quixotic heroes, of heart-warming Sancho Panzas and beauteous Dulcineas. The have all given us reasons to be grateful for the windows that television has opened for our generation. But they have also had the wit and the vision to see, and to remind us, that there are many other windows.

Nowadays we dare not be without the latest view of the world, brought to us by television. Nor dare we be without those other countless vistas which all civilization has prepared for us over the centuries—in books. This convergence we celebrate tonight.

A Time of Crisis in the Congress's Library, in the Nation's Library

Testimony before the Subcommittee on Legislative Appropriations, Committee on Appropriations, U.S. House of Representatives, February 20, 1986

Here Librarian Boorstin described in blunt language the severe effects that recent budget cuts were having on the Library. He also outlined the consequences of the Library's current requests being granted or not granted. In impassioned testimony, he implored Congress "to recognize that knowledge is not simply another commodity." Moreover, he warned, "historians will not fail to note that a people who could spend $300 billion on their defense . . . could not even keep their libraries open in the evening." Boorstin's strong plea, which earned him the sobriquet of "an intellectual Paul Revere," was well-received and resulted in the restoration of a substantial part of the sum that had been cut.

$\mathcal{M}$R. CHAIRMAN, and members of the committee. I want to thank you for this opportunity to appear before this committee to describe the needs of the Library and Congress for fiscal year 1987.

In the past on this occasion I have made a general statement and also filled in the outlines of our budgetary request with the figures for the several items. This morning, with the permission of the committee, I will follow another procedure. Because of the urgencies, which will appear as I go on, I will devote my statement to the large circumstances which explain our budgetary request, the significance of what we are asking for, and the consequences of our requests being granted, or not being granted.

I must warn the committee in advance that my statement, unlike all previous statements I have given to this friendly and generous committee, will sound an alarm. It is not, however, because I am an alarmist—whom the dictionary describes as "a person who habitually spreads alarming rumors, exaggerated reports of danger, etc." Quite the contrary. The Library of Congress has, I hope, acquired a reputation for honesty and conservatism in its requests to this committee, and in its projections for the future. This committee has always been sympathetic, and even generous, to the Library, and I like to think this is in part at least because we have done our bit, never asked for what we did not need, and always shared with your helpful staff suggestions as to how our requests might be prudently pared.

But this is not just another budget year. The situation of your—of our—Library is serious, it is even dangerous, and could become tragic for our nation, the Congress, and the whole world of learning. I would be failing in my oath of office if I did not take this opportunity to sound the alarm, and inform the committee as clearly and as honestly as I can of what is happening to your great Library, and what will happen if this committee—the only agency of our government with the power to act—does not act promptly.

Only fifteen months from now, during fiscal year 1987, the nation will begin to celebrate the bicentenary of our Constitution. Exactly 199 years ago, the Americans of the former colonies were selecting their delegates to the Constitutional Convention which opened with a quorum in Philadelphia on May 25, 1787. The most recent Library of Congress building was built by the Congress as a monument to James Madison, the leading chronicler of that meeting, and a principal architect of the Constitution. So that building, all the Library of Congress, our collections, and our staff—are dedicated to the proposition that free government is based on free, copious, and current access to knowledge. It would be a historic irony—the only analogy I can think of is the burning of the ancient Library of Alexandria in Egypt—if the Congress should choose this anniversary to direct and promote the disintegration of this great institution.

The greatest of republics has been served by the greatest of the world's libraries. But this will not continue to be possible, unless the Congress takes measures to repair the damage done and to be done by the vast and unprecedented cuts in the Library's budget. As the Librarian who has had a most cordial and respectful relation to this committee, I cannot help communicating to the committee some bafflement, sadness, and dismay from my colleagues at the Library, that the Library should have been singled out for a double dose of cuts this year, while some other libraries within the government have had their appropriations modestly increased. As this committee is aware, our regular budget for the current year had been cut by $8.4 million below that for the previous year even before current Gramm-Rudman-Hollings guidelines brought this cut to a total of more than $18 million.

Let me summarize the general consequences of these cuts, which foreshadow a tragic future ahead of us. Never before in peacetime have the following consequences ensued:

1. The nation's library will cease collecting needed current material.
2. Doors to the nation's library will be closed for lack of funds to provide normal security.
3. Hours of service will be curtailed, closing on Sundays and holidays, and all evenings except Wednesdays, making the Library's services and resources inaccessible to any person who must hold down a regular job.
4. Materials acquired will remain uncataloged and hence inaccessible.
5. Materials deteriorating for lack of treatment will not be preserved.

These are only a few of the disastrous consequences for the Congress, the nation, and the world of learning. This damage is accelerating, and to a considerable extent will be irreparable. These steps are abhorrent to us as citizens of a democratic nation. But I can assure you that we have spent more hours than I can count in meetings of our Library's staff devoted, not as I would have hoped, to discovering ways to be more serviceable to the Congress and to the nation, and to find rational and deliberate ways to secure economies—but rather to figure out how to meet the sudden demand for a Procrustes cut in each of our appropriations by an arbitrary percentage. How to find the least damaging ways to obey the law? The morale of our staff inevitably suffers. Not only from the need to dismiss some of our ablest people, but from the feeling that the excellence of this institution and its services goes unrecognized and unrewarded. We have become the bewildered victims of a mysterious numbers game.

This is then a time of crisis in your library, in Congress's library, in the nation's library. Yet for our nation and the world, these are the times that try men's minds, that tax our consciousness, our resources of wisdom, knowledge, and information. Threats from without and problems within demand every shred of the most ancient wisdom and the most recent information—to cope with the challenges of a nuclear war, to seize the opportunities of unprecedented technological progress, to enrich the resources of freedom. We, the greatest library on earth serving the greatest republic, are needed as never before by an imprisoned humanity. For many—perhaps most—peoples of the earth, those behind the Iron Curtain and in other enslaved nations, this Library remains the only place where they can freely learn about themselves.

This crisis has not been created by the Library of Congress. Our nation's library remains respected and envied worldwide. The crisis has not been created by inexpertise, neglect, waste, indolence, or dishonesty in the Library of Congress. It has been created by the Congress, the same institution and the same people who have built this great Library, and to whom it belongs before all others.

If the announced budgetary policy is pursued for the Library of Congress, the nation's library—your main resource of knowledge and information—will quickly deteriorate. It has taken two centuries to build this institution. It can be disintegrated in a decade and destroyed in two decades. And so it will be unless the fiscal policy toward the Library is repaired and reversed.

This greatest Library on earth—a monument to our Founders' faith in knowledge, a byproduct of our nation's faith in freedom of inquiry, will become a byword and a symbol of a nation's lack of faith in itself, a symptom of a nation in terror and decline. Historians will not fail to note that a people who could spend $300 billion on their defense would not spend $18 million on their knowledge—and could not even keep their libraries open in the evening. Historians will look with amazement and incredulity at a nation that could once afford to build grand structures bearing the names of Thomas Jefferson, John Adams, and James Madison—all lovers and champions of knowledge—yet decided it could no longer afford to acquire as effectively and abundantly as possible the current sources of knowledge. They will recall the last epoch of the Roman Empire when Romans were so fearful of the barbarians that they imitated the barbarians. These are not the priorities of civilization and freedom.

The two large retreats mandated on us by the Congress are both antidemocratic and antiknowledge. How can we justify or explain this to our people or to the world? Dare we say, simply, that our nation, perhaps the first nation on earth explicitly founded on knowledge, is now ready to disintegrate and destroy its own foundations? Knowledge is not a rock that we inherit from the geologic past, it is a living growing organism constantly in need of nourishment and renewal— the special task of your Library of Congress.

The disaster which I describe, the shame which will come on this nation if the Congress pursues a policy of disintegrating its library, can be averted only if this committee restores in our 1987 budget the cuts made in 1986, and keeps your Library thriving and growing, to keep pace with the progress of knowledge and the need for information. Of course, it is within the power of Congress to proceed as it wishes. But it is my sworn duty under the Constitution to alert the Congress to what it is doing, and use all my efforts to save the Congress and all of us from a historic disaster.

The Congress has become understandably suspicious of all claims for priority on our nation's public resources. We have been told that the "government" should only take on what the "government" can afford. But I would respectfully suggest that the "government" can afford nothing, not one bomber or aircraft carrier. It is the American people who can or cannot afford. And the Congress determines the priorities in expending what they provide. The fact that some claims of priority are ill-founded or bizarre does not mean that there are no priorities. The fact that "special interests" seek improper special consideration does not mean that there are no rational or patriotic priorities. Among these, alongside our nation's defense we must put our nation's knowledge. An ignorant nation, an incompletely informed Congress will not have the power to defend itself. Nor can a nation that undervalues knowledge hope to remain free.

I beg this committee to recognize that knowledge is not simply another commodity. On the contrary. Knowledge is never used up, it increases by diffusion, and grows by dispersion. Knowledge and Information cannot be quantitatively assessed, as a percentage of the GNP. Any willful cut in our resources of knowledge is an act of self-destruction.

I said at the outset that I am not an alarmist, but an honest person sounding the alarm. We have seen many groups march on Washington—farmers, advocates of school prayer, and many others—all witness to the constitutional freedom of all of us to petition our representatives in Congress. The strength—and the weakness—of the cause which I espouse on behalf of the Congress's Library and the World of Learning is precisely that we do not speak for any special interest or any one party or opinion. The cause of knowledge is the most general of all interests for a free people. The beneficiaries of knowledge, of the information supplied to Congress and the free explorers of knowledge, are everywhere. Their largest numbers are still unborn. We will fail in our duty to our posterity if we do not hand on to them the fully stocked, properly organized treasure of wisdom of the past which it has taken us two centuries to accumulate.

As a servant of the Congress, I beg this committee to do what it can to repair the damage being done by budgetary cuts. To restore your great resource of knowledge, your Library, to its stature, its progress, and its promise. My eloquent predecessor, during the last World War, described the Library of Congress as a Fortress of Freedom. There can be no more accurate description of our proper role, and the priority that your committee should help restore.

A Full-Time Citizen of the Republic of Letters

Statement by Daniel J. Boorstin announcing his
decision to step down as Librarian of Congress,
December 10, 1986

*Many observers had not expected Daniel Boorstin to stay at the
Library of Congress as long as twelve years. Nevertheless, his
announcement that he would step down on June 15, 1987, was
a surprise. His book The Discoverers, published in 1983, had
been a best-seller and, as he explained, he wanted more time to
write a companion volume and to lecture. His statement to the
staff included an assessment of his major accomplishments while
looking to the future: "We have developed a momentum for this
great institution which I hope my successor will continue."*

*I*NSTITUTIONS thrive with strong leadership, and they grow
with new leadership. There is no fixed term for the office
which I hold. Herbert Putnam served forty years; Archibald
MacLeish, five years. My predecessors have served various
periods as they thought best.

On June 15, 1987, I will have served nearly twelve years as
the Librarian of Congress. This has been the great experience
and the great opportunity of my life—to work with the
Congress, with you and our other colleagues at the Library,
with the librarians of the nation and the world, and to help
build this institution. It has been an inspiration to work with
people of such high devotion and varied skills. The public
service has given Ruth and me a sense of joy and fulfillment.
These have been full years.

I intend on next June 15 to step down from my post as
Librarian of Congress to become a full-time citizen of the

Republic of Letters. I will then have more time for writing and lecturing. Now I have begun writing a companion to *The Discoverers*, which will be called *The Creators*, and which I hope will not be my last book. I wish to do this not only in my off-hours.

These six months will give ample time for the nomination and confirmation of a successor, and for an orderly transition. In the next months I will, of course, continue to pursue energetically the purposes and projects of the Library. And after leaving the Librarian's Office I hope to continue to serve the Library, which so magnificently serves the Congress and the nation and the world of learning.

We can take satisfaction in what we have accomplished together in these last years. We have improved the services to Congress, extended the collections, widened the outreach to scholars and the whole community. We have sought the counsel of scholars on the collections and services of the Library, and we have opened the Library more than ever. We have tried to bring together the librarians and the library community of the world. We have found new ways to celebrate the book, to promote reading, to whet appetites for knowledge, and to make all our technologies—of the book, of television, of microforms, of the computer, of video and optical disk— complementary. We have led the way in the works of preservation. We have prepared the renewal and modernization of services in our Multi-Media Encyclopedia. With the generous help of the Congress we have begun renovation of our buildings so that the Library of Congress may remain in the next century a living monument to the faith of a free people in the quest for knowledge. We have developed a momentum for this great institution which I hope my successor will continue.

As a token of our love and admiration for the Library of Congress, in recognition of the Center for the Book, and to help it note the coming Year of the Reader, Ruth and I are making a gift to the Library of Congress of One Hundred Thousand Dollars to establish the Daniel J. and Ruth F. Boorstin Publications Fund. We hope others will follow our example.

Printing and the Constitution

Introduction to *Constitution of the United States:
Published for the Bicentennial of Its Adoption in 1787*
(Washington: The Library of Congress in association
with the Arion Press, San Francisco, 1987)

*The Librarian's essay on the Constitution focuses on the crucial
role of print in a democracy, particularly in the widespread diffusion
of the "most significant public facts." Our frame of government
"was born in the freedom to print and to read." Daniel Boorstin's
statement was prepared for a limited edition of the Constitution,
a typographic tribute to it, made by hand at the Arion Press in
San Francisco, sales of which benefited the Library of Congress.
An inexpensive paperbound facsimile edition was made available
by the Library through the Superintendent of Documents, U.S.
Government Printing Office.*

*T*HIS is a typographic tribute to the Constitution of the
United States. The nation's bicentennial celebration of the
framing of the Constitution will remind us that our flourishing
continent-wide federal union of fifty states is a byproduct of
this document. But this elegant printing of the Constitution
is a special kind of tribute—a celebration of something so
obvious, so omnipresent that it may be forgotten. Here is a
tribute to typography, "the art or process of printing from
type." We have been misled by the cliché that ours is the
oldest "written" constitution still in use. To be more precise
we should call ours probably the first *printed* constitution and
surely the oldest printed constitution by which a nation still
lives. This puts our Constitution in a wider, more modern
perspective.

Our nation was born in the bright light of history, and we can trace the framing and detailed revision of this document in the record of the Convention which met in Philadelphia from May 14 to September 17, 1787. Some of the members were men of letters, and all lived in a culture of printed matter. When the Consitutional Convention required a printer, they selected John Dunlap and David C. Claypoole, who had been printers to the Continental Congress since 1775. Their names had appeared on the official printing of the Declaration of Independence in 1776. They had proven their qualifications as the official printers of the Articles of Confederation.

The Framers believed that the strictest secrecy was required to encourage members of the Constitutional Convention to speak their minds freely and to remove temptations to demagoguery. Eleven years earlier, when once before the Continental Congress struggled to agree on a new form of government, they had sat in the same room where the Constitutional Convention now met. They then secured the signatures of Dunlap and Claypoole to an oath of secrecy: "We and each of us do swear that we will deliver all the copies of 'the articles of confederation' which we will print together with the copy sheet to the Secretary of Congress and that we will not disclose directly or indirectly the contents of the said confederation." The delegates to the new Constitutional Convention counted on their printers' observing a similar secrecy, and they were not disappointed.

As the work of the Convention drew toward a close and the Committee of Detail began putting the Convention's decisions into final form, Dunlap and Claypoole regularly supplied members with printed versions of the committee's latest revisions. The first printer's proofs went to the Committee of Detail about August 1 for additional changes. These were incorporated in corrected copy, distributed to all members of the Convention probably on August 6. A month later, in early September, the Convention as a whole made further revisions, which in turn were incorporated in a new version by the Committee of Detail. This was printed, and referred back to the Convention on September 12. "The report was then delivered in at the Secretary's table," recorded the Convention's Secretary William Jackson, "and having been once read throughout. Ordered that the Members be furnished with printed copies thereof. The draught of a letter to Congress being at the same time reported—was read once throughout, and afterwards agreed to by paragraphs." One September 14 and 15 the Convention went through this revised print section by section. On September 15 Madison noted, "On the question to agree to the Constitution as amended. All the States ay." George Washington wrote in his diary for that day that the Convention "adjourned 'till Monday that the Constitution which it was proposed to offer to the People might be engrossed—and a number of printed copies struck off." Dr. James McHenry of Maryland added in his diary that the order was for five hundred copies.

It is plain that in their efforts to give a final form in words to the concepts, arrangements, and compromises on which they had labored for four months, the members were always working with *printed* copy. They were continually adding their final changes to these printed versions of their draft Constitution. Only at the very end was their joint work finally reduced to "writing," by being "engrossed." This word *engross*, derived from the Medieval Latin for large handwriting, in this sense has left our common usage. It is seldom used now except for academic diplomas and certificates of award, wills, deeds, and other legal documents. Then it had a legalistic meaning: "to write out in a peculiar character appropriate to legal documents." By the late eighteenth century this common use of the word had already begun to become obsolete. Printing acquired a new authenticity. The framers of this historic legal document, in fashioning their crucial phrases, were using common printed matter and not a legalistic handwritten text. They were already working with a *printed* constitution.

How otherwise could the Convention have done its business, with fifty-five delegates conferring, consulting, debating, and agreeing on specific wording? For centuries the final form of historic political documents had been "engrossed," to be scrutinized by a few literate and technically competent negotiators. But this document was prepared in close consultation by fifty-five delegates. Could an original text have been reliably transcribed in fifty-five identical copies? Could members have been confident that they were all viewing precisely the same text? Posterity proved that any preposition, comma, colon, or capital letter might hold the fate of the commerce, general welfare, and international relations of a great nation. Without their printed copies they would have been at sea.

The later history of the document was an allegory of the primacy of print. In 1883 when J. Franklin Jameson, eminent American historian and bibliographer and sometime chief of the Manuscripts Division of the Library of Congress (1928-37), pursued the "engrossed" copies of our fundamental documents, he found that the engrossed copy of the Declaration of Independence was proudly and conspicuously displayed in the library of the Department of State in Washington. But there at the same time the engrossed handwritten Constitution of the United States "was kept folded up in a little tin box in the lower part of the closet." There was an unintended historic significance in this neglect of the handwritten word. For the gestation and adoption of the Constitution was not in the handwritten but in the printed word. The engrossed Constitution came to the Library of Congress in 1921, where it remained until 1952, when it went to the National Archives. Displayed in the rotunda, annually seen by hundreds of thousands, the handwritten version has finally attained the publicity of print.

There was a serious ambivalence, too, in the very word *engrossed*. During the Middle Ages it acquired a second meaning: "to buy up the whole stock of something for the purpose of establishing a monopoly." "Engrossing" in both sense is a relic of an old age of monopolies—in knowledge and power too. Printed matter announced a new age, not of "engrossing" but of diffusing.

A historic, and perhaps the first, example of the political implications of printing was the framing, the debating, and the adopting of our Constitution. While it was hardly conceivable that the fifty-five members of the Constitutional Convention could have done their work without the aid of the printing press, it was still less conceivable that without printing the people of thirteen newly independent colonies spread inland from fifteen hundred miles of Atlantic coast could have focused their minds and intelligently debated the document. The Federalist Papers and the other contemporary classics of political debate over the Constitution were themselves byproducts, as well as products, of the printing press. Of course, it was a printed version of the Constitution, of which we now provide an elegant reminder in the present volume, that then provided the common, public focus for their debates.

Unfortunately, Dunlap and Claypoole had to wait five years to be paid by the new government. Perhaps they were so patient because they had intended to do the job on speculation, hoping to profit from the public curiosity about what the secretive but much-publicized Convention had been up to. The Constitutional Convention had been, in James Hutson's apt phrase, "an extraordinary venture in confidentiality." Astonishingly, there were no significant leaks. In our age of "Sunshine" laws, when every private discussion in the councils of government is a potential headline or a feature of nightly newscasters, when every such council is not an intimate forum but a public sieve, it is worth reflecting whether the incomparable work of the Constitutional Convention could have been accomplished if they had been debating before journalists, newsmakers, and a public impatient for controversy and sensation.

The same Framers, who scrupulously observed their oaths of secrecy while they were deliberating, showed an admirable democratic concern that their product should, in George Washington's phrase, become an "offer to the People," that it be widely "promulged." The secrecy of their deliberation and the publicity of ensuing discussion were complementary. For centuries historic forces had inevitably confined the arena of interest and debate. Before the spread of literacy current access to earlier classics of constitutional history was inevitably limited to the small literate class. Magna Carta (1215), for example, could not have been debated by more than a tiny fragment of Britons, or even of barons, in its day. Written in Latin, a learned foreign language, the document survived in a few variant handwritten "originals" and entered British constitutional tradition more by rumor and hearsay than by public inspection. The Great Tradition of an "unwritten" British constitution left the knowledge and the scrutiny of the rights of Britons to judges and lawyers, rather than to the public.

The Constitution of the United States opened a new era in the history of constitutions, not only by its explicit description of the powers of a balanced representative government but also by its birth in a public forum of the printed word. A widely literate people could read and judge the very words by which they would be governed. The Constitution that emerged from the Philadelphia Convention in mid-September 1787, according to James Madison, "was nothing more than the draft of a plan, nothing but a dead letter, until life and validity were breathed into it by the voice of the people, speaking through the several State Conventions."

"Injunction of secrecy taken off. Members to be provided with printed copies," delegate McHenry noted in his diary on September 17, 1787, "Gentn. of Con. Dined together at the City Tavern." The Convention adjourned *sine die* at about four o'clock that afternoon. Secretary Jackson was then to carry copies of the Constitution to the Continental Congress (by now, the Congress of the Confederation) sitting in New York. That night Dunlap and Claypoole were under pressure to make minor revisions ordered at the last session of the Convention in time to have the printed copies ready for the New York stage leaving at ten the next morning. Just one hour later the Pennsylvania delegates were scheduled to present the document to their own legislature. The following afternoon Jackson arrived in New York to deliver the engrossed document and printed copies. On September 20 the Constitution was read to the Continental Congress.

Now at last the public could learn what had been accomplished by their fifty-five delegates who had worked for four months behind closed doors. The printing press would inform the public and bring the Constitution to life. Leonard Rapport's invaluable study of the early printings of the Constitution makes it possible for us to follow the role of the press in making the ensuing public debate possible. Without this diffusion of the printed text, the Constitution might conceivably still have been adopted by the required nine states. But the act never would have had the authority which copious printed publicity would ensure. The antifederalists had a plausible case for their objection that the Convention had exceeded its authority. Antifederalist sentiments were widespread. If copies of the Constitution had not been broadly diffused (how else if not in print?), this would have given substance to suspicions that the federalists were trying to overwhelm opposition by speed and surprise. In the result, however, full and accurate printed copies of the Constitution, broadcast by newspapers in every state, made it hard to argue that anyone had been deprived of the opportunity to object. Of course, the suffrage at the time was narrower than it is today. But in due course, literacy and other printed matter would play a role in changing that, too.

The general diffusion of printed texts of the new Constitution thus helped set a tone of fairness and decency, and declared the freedom to object, at the very adoption of our frame of government. Is it any wonder that Jefferson, who would take his lumps from the press, ventured that "the basis of our government being the opinion of the people, the very first object should be to keep that right; and were it left to me to decide whether we should have a government without newspapers, or newspapers without government, I should not hesitate a moment to prefer the latter." Unfortunately, Americans in the later twentieth century would see tragic allegories of Jefferson's point in great nations with powerful governments but no free newspaper press. They would see that, but for the freedom to print, there could be no "consent of the governed."

In September and October 1787, Americans learned about their proposed Constitution mainly through the newspaper press. The copies sent to the states for formal submission to their ratifying conventions, Leonard Rapport has shown, were actually produced as a newspaper supplement. In New York the twice-a-week *Independent Journal* published by John McLean, enthusiast for the new Constitution, regularly devoted three of its four pages to advertisements, and only the remaining page to news. To print the full text of the Constitution, he would have had to cut the advertisements. Therefore he printed the whole Constitution as a separate four-page *Supplement to the Independent Journal*, dated Saturday, September 22. To correct errors and omissions in his text he put the *Supplement* through three revisions and finally in a fourth revision added the resolutions of Congress of September 28 and the letter transmitting the report of the Convention of the states. Copies of this fourth version of the *Supplement*, attested by Charles Thomson, secretary of the Continental Congress, survive in the official archives of New York and North Carolina. It was on this printed version that the state ratifying conventions deliberated and cast their votes. There is good reason to dignify this *Supplement* to a semiweekly newspaper as "the printed archetype of the Constitution."

In the new age of typography it was not the uniqueness of an "engrossed" copy sequestered in some archive but the publicity of print that gave authenticity and authority to acts of government. Newspaper publishers were earnest, energetic, and ingenious in efforts to sate readers' appetites for the authentic product of the secretive Convention. On September 26 Benjamin Russell, publisher of the *Massachusetts Centinel*, offered the full text of the Constitution and boasted to his readers: "The following HIGHLY INTERESTING and IMPORTANT communication was received late last evening by the post—an ardent desire to gratify the patrons of the Centinel, and the publick in general, induced the Editor to strain a nerve that it might appear this day; and although lengthy he is happy in publishing the whole entire, for their entertainment." Nor did publishers allow profit to stand in their way. On September 28 the weekly Winchester *Virginia Gazette*, whose advertising revenues normally came to between six and eight dollars an issue, sacrificed all but one seventy-five cent advertisement to make space for the full text of the Constitution. The *New York Journal* of September 27 apologized to readers for omitting "a number of advertisements, pieces and paragraphs . . . to give place to the Federal Constitution," and so, too, did the Providence *United States Chronicle*.

It took some time for the printed word to get around. While newspaper versions speedily multiplied in the northeast and New England, it was Tuesday, October 2, before the printed text appeared south of Virginia. This was in an *Extraordinary*, a supplement to the semiweekly Charleston *Columbian Herald*, to which a ship had brought a copy of the text by an eleven-day passage from Philadelphia. On the remote frontier, in "the town of Lexington in the District of Kentucke," John Bradford's weekly *Kentucke Gazette* offered the full text of the Constitution in three installments beginning October 20.

Newspaper publishers tried various expedients. The *Norwich Packet* in Connecticut offered the text in two installments. The publisher of the *New-York Morning Post* and *Hutchins Improved Almanac* for 1788, advertised in the *Post* that a full four-page text of the Constitution was being inserted in his almanac, because it was "highly expedient" that everyone should have a copy of the proposed new Constitution, and "those who wish to possess themselves with one, have now an opportunity with the advantage of an Almanack into the Bargain." Others printed the Constitution in handbills and pamphlets.

Considering the length of the Constitution (more than five thousand words), the cost of hand-setting, the scarcity of paper, and the small size of newspapers at the time, to provide readers so promptly with the full text of so technical a document should demonstrate an impressive public spirit. Of about eighty newspapers publishing in the colonies at the time, by October 6, only twenty days after the Convention had adjourned, at least fifty-five had printed the full text. By the end of October the participating newspapers numbered some seventy-five. Even before Delaware, the first state, met in its ratifying convention on December 3, the number of separate printings of the Constitution in newspapers or other formats came (according to Rapport's count) to more than one hundred and fifty.

We can never know precisely how many printings were made of the full text of the Constitution before it was ratified. The multiplication of copies by print made knowledge more than ever uncontrollable, unaccountable, incalculable. The dissemination of print dramatized the mysterious powers of knowledge and its uncanny capacity to increase by diffusion. In a free American society the printing press made it possible for citizens to have access to the most significant public facts in privacy and at their convenience. Unlike a unique engrossed document, to which access could be controlled, printed copies spread with the wind. No one could know for sure who had read what, or when, or what any reader had found in it for himself. The multiplying copies of the *printed* proposed Constitution were symbols of an opening society in which eventually all would have a right to know and judge the public business.

The appearance in our dictionaries of the word *samizdat* in the mid-twentieth century to describe "dangerous" printed matter clandestinely circulated is an ominous reminder that some of the world's most powerful governments have retreated from the modern age of free public print to the dark age when public documents were "engrossed" for only a privileged few. Thomas Carlyle's familiar observation that the art of printing "was disbanding hired armies, and cashiering most kings and senates, and creating a whole new democratic order," is no longer a platitude. The story of the adoption of our Constitution can now more than ever remind us that our frame of government was born in the freedom to print and to read. That freedom has never been universal. In the year of the bicentennial of our Constitution the world more than ever needs the historic example of the vitality of a government founded in the judgment of citizens—free to print and to read.

The printed publicity of the debate over the Constitution carried still another historic message. As Dunlap and Claypoole and McLean printed and corrected their successive versions of the text, they were reminded that its words were the work of fallible men. The odor of sanctity, the aura of divinity, the historic inevitability that despots have always claimed for their self-serving laws, were being dissolved. Men were here reminded of their responsibility for their laws, their powers to make and shape their own constitution. What men had made, they could improve. The explicit provision for amendment, a characteristically American feature, proved essential to the longevity of our Constitution. Printing the Constitution reminded men that their laws were not the creation of a uniquely sacred "engrossing" legal hand, but the product of public information and agreement to what everybody could know.

Public print, especially newspaper-print, was the clearest testimony that the institutions of government were only human, always improvable, and so always perfectible. In this bicentennial year, sharing this hope, we hear Benjamin Franklin's wise advice at the close of the Constitutional Convention: "Thus I consent, Sir, to this Constitution, because I expect no better, and because I am not sure it is not the best. The opinions I have had of its errors I sacrifice to the public good. . . . I hope, therefore, for our own sakes, as a part of the people, and for the sake of our posterity, that we shall act heartily and unanimously in recommending this Constitution, wherever our influence may extend, and turn our future thoughts and endeavors to the means of having it well administered."

To Free Us from Our Technological Traffic Jam

Statement on behalf of a joint resolution to authorize
and request the President to call a White House
Conference on Library and Information Services,
Committee on Labor and Human Resources,
U.S. Senate, April 3, 1987

Boorstin's testimony before the Senate Committee on Labor and Human Resources reiterated many of the themes he had emphasized for the previous twelve years, particularly the need to "reawaken our nation to the neglected priority of books and reading and all our knowledge-institutions." The urgent task, in 1987 as well as in 1975, was "to bring together all technologies," including television, the computer, and the book, in the service of a more literate, enlightened, and joyful America. This address was Daniel J. Boorstin's last major statement as Librarian of Congress. The date of his departure was delayed until September 14, 1987, when his successor, James H. Billington, took the oath of office as the thirteenth Librarian of Congress. On that day Daniel J. Boorstin became Librarian of Congress Emeritus and "a full-time Citizen of the Republic of Letters."

I WOULD LIKE TO SPEAK in behalf of Senate Joint Resolution 26, a joint resolution to authorize and request the President to call a White House Conference on Library and Information Services. I am here to voice some cautions and to offer some suggestions on how such a conference may best serve well our urgent national cultural needs.

When any group of professionals meets, they are understandably tempted to talk to one another and to emphasize the latest problems of their profession rather than the interests of the public for whom they exist.

Librarians, whose professional organization, the American Library Association, came into existence in 1876, only a little over a century ago, have a long, proverbial, and honorable tradition. They have been servants of civilization, agents of literacy, counselors of the young, and helpers of all who would educate themselves. But the swift progress of American technology, especially library and information technology, in which the Library of Congress has played a leading role, has itself created new problems. It is perhaps no accident that the spectacular advance and popularity of information technology has been accompanied by a lapse of literacy and a decline in the disposition to read books among several segments of our population.

A national study, by the Center for the Book in the Library of Congress at the instruction of the Congress, produced a report entitled *Books in Our Future*, issued by the Joint Committee on the Library in 1984. This report collected the disturbing evidence of the prevalence of illiteracy (the inability to read) and aliteracy (the reluctance or unwillingness to read). The national survey of reading habits by the Book Industry Study Group released in 1983 revealed that 44 percent of adult Americans who could read had not read a book in the preceding six months. Even more alarming, among Americans under twenty-one years of age who could read, it was found that those who had read a book in the previous year declined from 75 percent in 1978 to 62 percent in 1983. Especially discouraging, the report of 1983 found only 29 percent who had read a book within the previous six months. The surveys did confirm that the reading of books is greatest among children whose parents read books. The survey by the Department of Education, *A Nation at Risk*, found that the nation has at least twenty-three million adults who are functionally illiterate.

We must not forget Thomas Jefferson's warning that "if a nation expects to be ignorant and free . . . it expects what never was and never will be." The printed book, our most ancient liberating technology, still challenges our energies and ingenuity if we are to reap its democratizing benefits. The statistics I have just cited show how far we still have to go.

When the last White House Conference on Library and Information Services met in 1979, the conference did not emphasize books and reading and the problems of illiteracy but instead focused sharply on the new technologies of information storage and retrieval and on the needs of special constituencies. At the final session I seized the opportunity to alert librarians and others to the dangers of allowing these new technologies to distract us from the unfulfilled opportunities of the technologies of the book. I reminded the conference of the crucial distinction between knowledge (the special realm of the book) and information (the special realm of the media and the newer technologies of communication). And I warned of the perils of our becoming an Information-Society rather than a Knowledgeable Society.

The newer technologies of information storage and retrieval have flourished and advanced spectacularly in the last decade. The Library of Congress, with the generous support of the Congress, has been a leader in this advance. We have pioneered in applying the computer to bibliographic control, and in exploring the benefits of the optical disk and the video disk.

In the nation as a whole we see the information industry flourishing. But our knowledge-institutions go begging. The percentage of U.S. dollars going to the information industry continues to grow while our educational system erodes and our major research institutions are in dire need. A new White House Conference could conceivably give hope to our librarians, scholars, educators, and all enlightened citizens. It could reawaken the nation to the neglected priority of books and reading and all our knowledge-institutions.

Librarians have been understandably tempted to become information technologists instead of guides to the world of knowledge and the delights of the literary arts. Fortunately, these need not be exclusive alternatives. But there is danger now that a misplaced emphasis will make them seem so.

This a familiar American temptation—to be so fascinated

by the new technology that we do not see its perils. Delight in the new is one of the most appealing features of our American character, the continuing promise of this Still-New-World. A parable of our thinking on the frontiers of technology is the story, perhaps apocryphal, of Henry Ford's conversation with a friend when he was just beginning to put thousands of Model T's on the road. "Mr. Ford," the friend asked, "Won't your speedy noisy horseless carriages make a lot of trouble, cause accidents, and create chaos by frightening all the horses?" Henry Ford had a quick response. "Not at all, my friend. Everybody will have an automobile—there won't be any horses on the roads. Then there won't be any problem!" Henry Ford could not imagine that with his horseless carriage he was inventing a new problem. And all of us on the clogged highways know that this is a problem to which we have not yet found a solution.

There has never yet been a technology invented to solve a problem which did not itself become part of the problem. The computer technology and microchip and the laser magic of storage and retrieval are not likely to be an exception. Let us beware!

There are some special reasons, too, why our library profession has become enchanted, even mesmerized, by the magic of the newer technology. Until recently, when women were denied equal opportunities for fulfillment in other professions, they were perforce channeled into schoolteaching, nursing—and librarianship. They were refused access to the mechanical, the engineering, and the high-tech professions. Movies still being replayed remind us of that stereotype—the unlipsticked librarian—lady with her hair in a bun, acting the gentle samaritan to the young and the lonely in the community.

Computer technology, information technology, has offered a welcome opportunity to change this stereotype. Librarianship, even in small libraries, has become mechanized in new ways. The librarian's work, no longer imprisoned in an obsolete gentility, has found its bold new place on the honorific frontiers of science and technology. Now in libraries, our information-engineers, like any other technicians, have their arcane vocabulary, and a respectably elaborate machinery, just as likely as any other to get out of order and to need expert attention. Ironically, this new technology has become a symbol of the liberation and invigoration of library science.

This is not to deny that the computer technology can and does accomplish bibliographic miracles, offering magical guidance to scholar and scientist. The work of cataloging is being purified of dehumanizing routine. Access to books and to bits of information in any conceivable category is available with astonishing speed. Once information or images have been put into the computer, or onto the optical disk or the video disk, the scholar has an Aladdin's lamp. We at the Library of Congress have done everything in our power to apply these new technologies and spread the word of their uses for scholars and legislators and citizens.

But we must not allow ourselves to be dazzled by the prospects of the latest technology. Even if literacy ceases to be fashionable, the book has not become obsolete. And literacy remains the tonic of our democracy.

While our nation, unlike others, has no national library system, we have the most effective and most comprehensive public libraries in the world. Our Nation of Readers, of self-made leaders, has been fostered by our 8,300 community public library systems. Their strength, like that of our public schools, has come from the grassroots. And they too have become a distinctively American tradition, created and enriched by the book-inspired vision of Andrew Carnegie, Julius Rosenward, and thousands of other citizen-philanthropists. They have been nourished by the warm devotion and expertise of librarians. They are, of course, a by-product of the technology of the printed word—aided by the increasing facilities of electric light and central heating and air-conditioning.

And in our machine-ridden society the public library has been an asylum from automation, from noise, and from haste. "Literature is my utopia," said Helen Keller; "Here I am not disenfranchised." The library is everybody's utopia, where, as Ezra Pound reminded us, we read the "news that stays news."

In the last few years, I have visited impressive new library buildings where, at the inauguration ceremonies, I am shown the latest electronic systems of storage and retrieval and introduced to the designers of the system. But I often must ask, with embarrassment, to be shown the books. I begin to fear that our libraries, like our highways, are threatened by a technological traffic jam.

If there is to be White House Conference on this crucial area of American life, it should be charged with keeping all our technologies in an effective and amiable alliance. The Congress ten years ago created the Center for the Book in the Library of Congress for precisely this purpose. The Congress has declared 1987 to be the Year of the Reader. For this, too, is the Bicentennial of our Constitution, which was conceived by men who read books, in the image of a knowledgeable citizenry.

The White House Conference should be renamed a Conference on Literacy, Books, Libraries, and Information Services. The conference should aim to free us from our technological traffic jam. It should help us bring together all technologies— television, the computer, and the book, in the service of a more enlightened and more joyful, because more literate, America.

Daniel J. Boorstin: A Biographical Note

Daniel J. Boorstin was Librarian of Congress from 1975 to 1987. He had previously served as Director of the National Museum of History and Technology (1969–1973) and then as Senior Historian of the Smithsonian Institution in Washington, D.C. To come to the Smithsonian, he left his position as Preston and Sterling Morton Distinguished Service Professor of History at the University of Chicago, where he had taught for twenty-five years.

Born in Atlanta, Georgia, and raised in Tulsa, Oklahoma, Dr. Boorstin received his undergraduate degree with highest honors from Harvard College and his doctorate from Yale. As a Rhodes Scholar at Balliol College, Oxford, England, he won a coveted "double first" in two degrees in law and was admitted as a barrister-at-law of the Inner Temple, London. He has been visiting professor at numerous institutions: the University of Rome; Kyoto University, Japan; the University of Puerto Rico; the Sorbonne, University of Paris, where he was the first incumbent of a chair in American History; the Graduate Institute of International Studies, University of Geneva, Switzerland; and Cambridge University, England, where he was Pitt Professor and Fellow of Trinity College. Cambridge University awarded him its D. Litt. degree in 1968. He has lectured widely in the United States and all over the world. Daniel Boorstin is married to the former Ruth Frankel and they have three sons.

Among Daniel J. Boorstin's many publications are the trilogy *The Americans: The Colonial Experience* (1958), which won the Bancroft Prize, *The Americans: The National Experience* (1965), which won the Parkman Prize, and *The Americans: The Democratic Experience* (1973), which won the Pulitzer Prize for History and the Dexter Prize; and *The Discoverers* (1983). Other books by Daniel Boorstin include *The Mysterious*

Science of the Law (1941), *The Lost World of Thomas Jefferson* (1948), *The Genius of American Politics* (1953), *America and the Image of Europe* (1960), *The Image* (1962), *The Decline of Radicalism* (1969), *The Sociology of the Absurd* (1970), *Democracy and Its Discontents* (1974), *The Exploring Spirit* (1976), *The Republic of Technology* (1978), *A History of the United States* (1980), with Brooks M. Kelley, and the two-volume *Landmark History of the American People* for young readers, with Ruth F. Boorstin, which was revised and updated in 1987. He has served as editor of *Delaware Cases, 1792-1830* (1943), *An American Primer* (1966), *American Civilization* (1971), and the thirty-volume series, the Chicago History of American Civilization.

This book, which was designed by James E. Conner, was typeset in Zapf International and Zapf Chancery by Monotype Composition Company, Baltimore, Maryland, and printed by Garamond Pridemark Press, Baltimore. The binding was done by American Trade Bindery, Columbia, Maryland. The paper is acid-free Mohawk Superfine.